AVALANCHE OF SPIRITS:

THE GHOSTS OF WELLINGTON

BY KAREN FRAZIER

Avalanche of Spirits: The Ghosts of Wellington

By Karen Frazier

Cover photograph by Patty Valdez

Copyright © 2013 Karen Frazir

ISBN-13: 978-1482396683

ISBN-10: 1482396688

10 9 8 7 6 5 4 3 1

10 9 8 7 6 5 4 3 2 1

To the people who loved the town of Wellington so much they lingered, those who lost their lives in tragedy but remained, and the living, who return time and time again so that those left behind will be remembered.

Foreword

A few years ago, in 2009, I visited the ghost town of Wellington, Washington for the first time. It was a profoundly life-changing experience. Before I visited Wellington, I remained agnostic about the existence of ghosts, so much so, I was in the process of writing a book discussing all of the reasons for my agnosticism.

July 11, 2009, and the summer and fall that followed changed all that forever. From the moment I stepped into the parking lot at Wellington, I felt drawn and connected in a way I had never experienced before, nor have I experienced since. Wellington changed me.

That winter, I sat down and wrote a book called *Avalanche of Spirits: The Ghosts of Wellington*. The book was a love letter to a place that profoundly changed me. As I later learned, Wellington affected many others as well.

Since writing *Avalanche of Spirits: The Ghosts of Wellington*, my relationship with the railroad town has matured. In many ways, Wellington has become the happy place I go to commune, not only with the spirits I continue to believe inhabit the location, but also to see living people that have become family in just a few short years.

My experiences with Wellington did not end with *Avalanche of Spirits: The Ghosts of Wellington*. They remain ongoing. As I write this, it is late spring in Western Washington. Wellington has been largely inaccessible to us all winter, an experience that brings a nostalgic longing for those of us who make it our second home every summer. Winter has been harsh along the West Coast this year, the result of the La Niña oceanic atmospheric condition that creates cooler weather, bigger storms, and way too much snow in the mountains. It appears our annual return to Wellington will be later this year than ever.

Still, the ghost town is never far from my mind. It remains entrenched. I eagerly await the moment I am able to return to walk the beautiful mountainous trail that meanders through its heart.

Karen Frazier
June 10, 2011
Chehalis, Washington

Part I: A Spark Ignites

A Love Letter to Wellington
(November 26, 2009)

I'm sitting amidst the ruins of a documentary film I worked on for hundreds of hours and spent thousands of dollars to make. Like this book, the film was to be called *Avalanche of Spirits: The Ghosts of Wellington.*

The documentary was a way for me to tell a story that captivated me from the moment I first heard of it: the story of Wellington, Washington, the avalanche that claimed at least 96 lives, and the ghosts who remain there 100 years after the tragedy.

The project came to a screeching halt for many reasons. I would say it was mostly because of creative differences. It was nobody's fault really. If there was a failure, it was mine. In my optimism and excitement at sharing the story of Wellington, I failed to notice there might be others who didn't share my vision.

I am feeling great loss and sadness. I am grieving. It is because I love Wellington. With all my heart, I do. The documentary was my love letter to Wellington. It was a "thank you" to the spirits there. They have changed my life in innumerable ways.

There are ghosts at Wellington, and I gave them my word I would share their story. It is a story people need to hear so they can remember the ghosts there.

For me, the documentary was never about fame or fortune. I knew neither would follow. Instead, it was a story that came from my heart. It was a love letter to a place that calls to me when I am not there.

Here I sit. The documentary is in shambles. I showed the rough cut to friends today, and I cried as I watched. I have a promise to keep. This movie won't be it.

Yet, as my friend Leslie told me after watching the movie, "You have to tell this story."

I agree. I do.

I was mourning the documentary yesterday when my husband Jim said to me, "Would you trade a moment of your experiences? If you knew from the beginning that this would be the outcome, would you still have spent all that time at Wellington?"

The answer is a resounding yes. I loved every minute I spent there. I also loved every moment spent at my computer taking raw footage and crafting it into a story honoring Wellington, its spirits, and the investigators who return every summer. I loved the time I spent talking to the investigators and hearing their stories. I wouldn't have changed a minute of it. Knowing what I know now, I would still go back and do it all again without hesitation.

All things happen for a reason. I can't help but believe a door has opened. It is up to me to walk through it, and I have a promise to keep. I promised the ghosts I would share their story, and I shall in the way I know best. By writing about Wellington, I can honor all of those who love it as I do — ghosts and humans alike.

In the Beginning (February 2009)

It all began with a picture, which drew me into the story of Wellington. I had never heard of Wellington, Washington, until one evening when I was conducting an interview with a local paranormal group, Washington Anomalies Research (WAR). I asked for the group's single best piece of evidence, and they told me about the picture.

Taken on the observation deck of a rails-to-trails project in Washington State's Cascade Mountain Range, the photo shows a bright blue glowing swirl, extending up to the sky like angel's wings. Coming out of the bottom, you can see what appears to be a cuffed pant leg and a boot.

That was my introduction to Wellington.

Unfortunately, it was winter and impossible to reach Wellington, which sits buried under deep snowdrifts from November until the spring thaw in June or beyond. From that moment, however, Wellington called me. I felt a connection to a place I had never visited for reasons I couldn't fathom.

I have never really been sure about the existence of ghosts. I certainly wanted to believe they existed. Some early experiences made me wonder if ghosts were real, but my scientific bent always blocked me from belief.

Then I went to Wellington. After a short time there, I not only became convinced about the existence of ghosts, but I was also about to embark on a very personal journey that led me to greater faith and a stronger understanding of the human soul.

Wellington has changed me profoundly. To go from not knowing to knowing about the existence of ghosts and the human soul removes a great deal of fear. While I've never had an oppressive fear of death, I certainly find the apprehension about the unknown disconcerting.

I spent my summer and fall at Wellington. From July through late October 2009, I returned repeatedly. Something there kept drawing me back. I couldn't explain it. I loved the breathtaking beauty of the mountain location, the anomalous activity that takes place there, and the story of the tragedy that occurred a century ago in 1910, but there was something more.

Wellington has an energy that calls to me. Whenever I make the three-hour drive from my house to Wellington and the Iron Goat Trail in the Cascade Mountains, I can feel that energy drawing me closer.

The energy is not the only thing that keeps me returning. It is also my love for the spirits there. Unable to retain my journalist's detachment and impartiality, I have fallen in love with my subject.

As fall turned into winter, the snow came to Wellington. Now the road to Wellington is inaccessible, and three hours away might as well be three million miles. Still, Wellington calls to me. I will be going about my day when I feel a familiar tickle around the edges of my mind. It is   Wellington. The ghosts are there, living out the winter and awaiting the return of their human companions.

What started with a picture has become a lifelong love affair with a place to which I will return again and again.

Part II: What Happened at Wellington

King Railroad (February 22, 1910)

It was late February 1910, and the railroad was king. It had the ability to build empires. Towns that fell along railroad lines prospered. In the newly booming Pacific Northwest, Seattle won the battle of the railroad and became the western terminus of the northernmost railroad line in the United States.

Owned by the Great Northern Railway (GNR), the Northern rail line ran across the craggy Cascade Mountain range through the 4,056-foot-high pass discovered by GNR locating engineer John Stevens in the 1890s.

During the winter months, mounds of snow frequently buried the tracks through Stevens Pass. Due to the diligence of the rail line digging crews — made up of mostly immigrant labor working under the watchful eye of GNR superintendent James O'Neill — no train ever stalled for more than 24 hours in the snowy peaks of the North Cascade Mountains.

It was with the confidence of this knowledge that on the evening of February 22, 1910, 55 passengers boarded Spokane Local No. 25 to take the snowy journey across Eastern Washington through the Cascade Mountains and into Seattle, Washington.

The passengers were on the train for disparate reasons. Edward Topping traveled to recover from the recent death of his young wife. The Beck family, consisting of George and Ella and their three children — Harriet (6), Erma (4 ½), and Leonard (nearly 3)

— were returning to their home in California after trying to make a life in Marcus, Washington, where they found the harsh winters too much to bear. George Davis and his daughter Thelma were traveling after burying Thelma's mother in Spokane. Nellie Sharp was a recent divorcée who was headed west as a reporter documenting her travels for *McClure's Magazine*. Ida Starrett boarded the train with her three children — Lillian (9), Raymond (7), and Francis (8 months) — as well as her parents, Mr. and Mrs. May, who were taking the family home to British Columbia following the death of Mr. Starrett in late December.

These were just a few of the passengers boarding the westbound train, which would travel along the 375-mile route through the snowy flats of Eastern and Central Washington during a late winter blizzard.

The train chugged through the snowy night, followed closely by Fast Mail Train No. 27 from St. Paul, Minnesota. The mail train made haste in the wake of Local No. 25, because weather in Idaho held it up and the mail needed to get through.

At home on the West side in Everett, Washington, Superintendent James O'Neill watched the weather warily. It had been a rough winter, unlike any O'Neill had previously experienced as a superintendent for GNR. All winter, O'Neill waged a battle against heavy snows and voluminous slides blocking the tracks through the mountains. The weather stretched his digging crews thin as they kept the lines clear.

Now O'Neill faced a new challenge. A storm was rapidly approaching the North Cascades, but O'Neill had the confidence of experience telling him that this storm would be just like any other and that delays would be as manageable as they had been all winter.

O'Neill was a thorough and hardworking superintendent, and he decided to take his personal train to the railroad town of Wellington at Stevens Pass in order to strategize on location as the storm developed.

Wellington was a tiny town sitting along a ridge near the apex of Stevens Pass. The town existed for the railroad, and its hearty residents forged a life in which they spent nearly seven months a year under the snow. During that time, snow effectively cut the town off from the rest of the world. The only access to the outside world was by train and via telegraph lines, which heavy snow frequently felled.

Wellington perched along a ridge sitting above Tye Creek, and trains passed along tracks running across a narrow ledge cut into the edge of the mountainside.

While the town had a few families as permanent residents, many more were transient railroad workers who lived in GNR bunkhouses and commercial boarding houses in the town.

When O'Neill arrived at Wellington, he parked his private car along a passing spur track tucked in at the base of a snowy hill. He got straight to work, directing the four rotary snowplows attempting to keep the   tracks clear of snow. In the event the snow was too deep for the rotary plows, crews remained on hand to dig deep drifts from the tracks so rotaries could finish the job.

O'Neill was as ready as he could be for whatever winter in the Cascades had to throw at him.

Entangled in Ice (February 23–24, 1910)

A t 1 a.m. on February 23, Local No. 25 and Fast Mail Train No. 27 stopped at the small town of Leavenworth on the east side of Stevens Pass, awaiting orders from O'Neill about whether the tracks provided a safe passage through the mountains.

It had been snowing all night, but the passengers on the train had no reason to suspect when they went to sleep they would awaken anywhere but in Seattle. Two eastbound trains and one westbound train made it safely through the passes earlier. At approximately 1:30 a.m., O'Neill ordered the two trains to proceed from Leavenworth into the mountains. They headed west toward the Cascade Tunnel, which sat at the apex of the Pass and tunneled through the 2 ½ miles between the Cascade Station at its eastern terminus and Wellington to the west.

By 2 a.m., crews attached helper engines to both trains, and they headed up into the mountains behind a rotary snowplow that was clearing away new snow.

At the same time, another rotary snowplow left Wellington and traveled west to prepare the way for the two trains as they passed down out of the mountains and into the flats of Western Washington. The plow passed through several areas where the walls of previously plowed snow had caved in and easily cleared away a small slide.

About a mile and a half out of Wellington, just before reaching Windy Point — a dangerous spot in which the tracks clung to the side of the mountain over a precipitous drop to the town of Scenic, nearly 1,000 feet below — the plow encountered a slide that rose well above the reach of its blades. Attempting to chew through the snow, the rotary stuck in the ice and snow, and no shovelers were present to free it.

With conditions worsening on the western slope of the mountains, Superintendent O'Neill decided to stop the two trains on the east end of the Cascade Tunnel at the Cascade Station. Both trains pulled onto passing tracks, awaiting the "all clear" from O'Neill.

The all clear didn't come for two days.

Cascade Station wasn't a town. It was a small stop along the railroad existing to support the Cascade Tunnel. Along with a tiny feeding shack for the train crews called the Beanery, there were a few buildings supporting track switching and eastside control of the tunnel.

Since there was no place to go, the passengers and crew remained on the trains trying to pass the time, mostly by complaining of the delay that kept them from their business on the western side of the state. There were several children on the train, including the three Beck children, the three Starrett children, three-year-old Thelma Davis, and 18-month-old Varden Gray. The adults tried to keep the children as busy as they could through the long hours of confinement.

Shovelers worked diligently, digging the snow as it piled up around the trains in order to keep the trains from freezing to the tracks and ready to move at any moment.

At mealtimes, the passengers bundled up and hiked to the tiny Beanery, where they ate the food prepared by the cook and his assistant. Many of the well-heeled passengers expressed dismay they had to eat alongside the rail workers, who some considered "the scum of the Earth." Having so many extra mouths to feed quickly taxed the small Beanery's supply of food.

For two days, the passengers fretted as the snow continued to fall. Finally, news came the trains were moving through the tunnel to Wellington. It took the two trains hours to prepare for the short trip through the tunnel, and at 8 p.m. on February 24, a rotary snowplow led local No. 25 through the Cascade Tunnel and onto the passing tracks in the tiny town of Wellington. The Fast Mail Train soon followed.

A strong wind kicked up in the mountains that night, blowing snow into drifts around the two trains as they sat perched on the passing tracks just west of Wellington.

Because of the large rotary and line crews, who were now at Wellington to help get the trains through the snow, there were few bunk facilities available. Resultantly, many railroad employees wound up finding extra space to bunk for the night on the two trains.

In spite of keeping a close eye on the conditions, O'Neill and his men had no clue how far west the trains could get without running into slide conditions again. The rotary plows almost made it to Windy Point before encountering slides, which was fewer than two miles west of Wellington and still high up in the mountains. Snow buffeted the mountains, and the danger of avalanche steadily increased along the line on the western slopes of the Cascades.

Shortly before midnight, a rotary snowplow headed west to attempt to clear the line so that the trains could get through. It didn't make it very far.

More Bad News (February 25–27, 1910)

Much as they had for the past few days, the passengers awakened on the morning of February 25 to a world of white. Moving the trains to Wellington hadn't changed the scenery much, although now Local No. 25 sat perched along the walls of a V-shaped canyon under a 2,000-foot slope and above a 100-foot drop to Tye Creek below.

In summer 1909, a raging forest fire had deforested the half-mile-long slope above the passing tracks. Now it loomed 2,000 feet above the trains, bare of trees. It was a daunting wall of white.

Bad news greeted the passengers that morning. During the night, an avalanche had swept down the slope above Cascade Station and knocked out the Beanery, killing the cook and his assistant. Now, the threat of an avalanche seemed a very real possibility to the passengers, who warily eyed the slope above. The passengers were somewhat reassured, however, by the knowledge an avalanche had never before occurred in that location.

On the snow front, Superintendent O'Neill was fighting a war. Like a good general leading a charge, he used all of his resources to clear the lines to the west so the trains could continue through. Plow and shovel crews worked around the clock, digging in wet, heavy, debris-laden snow. The men only slept intermittently, stopping for a meal and a few minutes of sleep before returning to the backbreaking labor. Unfortunately, the weather fought them at every turn. Slides continuously came down along the lines, snow fell at alarming rates, and rotary plows either got stuck or were able to get through only to have to move on to a new slide in a new spot.

To top it off, some temporary laborers shoveling the lines to make way for the rotary snowplows decided to organize a revolt. Unhappy with the paltry wages earned, they demanded an astronomical immediate pay raise or they would stop working. When the GNR supervisors refused to negotiate, many walked off the job, leaving O'Neill with even less manpower than before.

Not one to command from the sidelines, O'Neill spent hours in the wet and cold alongside his men doing whatever it took to clear the tracks. At the same time, he had the weight of decision making on his shoulders, and he was aware the two trains were experiencing the longest delay ever in the Cascade Mountains. His priorities were clearing the tracks, getting the trains through to the West Coast, keeping his passengers safe, and communicating with the railroad.

In the town of Wellington, the passengers disembarked from the trains a few times a day to eat dinner at the Bailets Hotel. In the tiny town, the hotel was the only place for lodging or dining, and it shared a common façade with the few other businesses that supported the town: a saloon and a general store.

As O'Neill waged his war, the passengers on the train grew restless. Many demanded a meeting with O'Neill to discuss the situation; however, the superintendent was too busy fighting on the front lines to have time for a sit-down, leaving the passengers dissatisfied.

Soon, they began asking Local No. 25's conductor, Joseph Pettit, whether they might be in danger, perched as precariously as they were beneath a wall of snow over a drop-off. They asked Pettit to move the trains back to Leavenworth to wait out the storm. Pettit assured the passengers that they were perfectly safe where they were, telling them the area above the passenger tracks was not prone to avalanches and, in fact, had never slid. While Pettit spoke the truth, he also faced another reality. Even if he'd wanted to move the trains back to Leavenworth, he couldn't. Wellington was running short of coal, which was necessary to power the engines and snowplows fighting the slides, as well as the engine attached to Local No. 25. Slides to the east and the west further prevented significant movement of either train.

Pettit's reassurances did little to calm the passengers. The avalanche at the Cascade Station worried them, and many begged him to pull the trains back into the tunnel, where they felt that they would be safe.

The tunnel was no safer than the passing tracks. Many passengers on moving coal trains suffocated over the years as they passed through the Cascade Tunnel, and moving Local No. 25 there would necessitate turning off the burners that heated and supplied power to the trains. In the tunnel, the passengers risked either asphyxiation or hypothermia. On the passing tracks, they risked avalanche. Further complicating the issue, a coal shortage rendered moving the trains impossible. Local No. 25 and the Fast

Mail Train stayed where they were.

The passengers settled in to spend another night in Wellington.

The morning of February 26 dawned with no news, other than the fact the tiny town was running low on food and everyone would need to begin rationing so that they didn't run out.

Rotary crews were off to the west. They'd managed to get past the slide at Windy Point before having to return for more coal. Now they were headed west again to see if the tracks were clear beyond Windy Point.

All day, the passengers waited for the news the trains could finally begin to move. Unfortunately, late in the day, the rotary plow returned with bad news. Another slide had come down at Windy Point. The trains were still trapped.

The rotary plow worked on the new slide for most of the day, until it was time to return for more coal. As it headed back east toward Wellington, it came across a huge slide in the area of snow shed 3.3. Now there was no access to the coal supply and a huge slide ahead to clear before they could get to it.

Word got back to the passengers about this new slide. All of the rotary plows were now out of commission. There seemed very little chance that the trains would make it out of the mountains until the storm stopped.

Down but not out, O'Neill returned to Wellington. Earlier, the storm knocked out the telegraph wires in town. Wellington was effectively cut off from the   rest of the world.

O'Neill formulated a new plan. At first light, he would hike down the track to the Scenic Hot Springs Resort, where he could use the telegraphs to coordinate new rotary plows from other places along the GNR line.

Early in the morning of February 27, James O'Neill strapped on snowshoes and headed west toward Scenic along the railway line. He took two employees with him. On Local No. 25, a group of passengers heard of O'Neill's hike, and decided to attempt it themselves. They set out a few hours behind O'Neill, promising to send word back about conditions along the line.

The going was slow, and the men had to struggle their way through blockages and slides, but they managed the hike to Windy Point. From there, there was nothing to do but slide down a steep 800-foot slope to the resort town below.

When the passengers reached Scenic, they encountered O'Neill and his men, who told them the story about how one of the men had been swept away by sliding snow during the hike, only to appear later at the resort. The passengers stayed in Scenic, but O'Neill returned to Wellington carrying a message to those remaining on the train: "Arrived safely. Do not come."

As day turned into night, those on the train awaited word from their fellow passengers. Had they reached Scenic safely? Was the trail passable? With food and coal shortages looming, the passengers were more than anxious to escape from their snowy dungeon.

GNR employees and passengers all prepared to spend another night on the edge of the mountain.

The Roar of Nature (February 28–March 1, 1910)

As another morning dawned on the mountain, little progress occurred toward the ultimate goal of getting the trains safely down the western slope of the Cascades.

Frustration and fear continued to mount among the passengers, until another group decided to not await fate, trying their luck at hiking out. If the trail was passable, they would send word back to Local No. 25, and those who remained would arrange for evacuation. Surely, the passengers reasoned, hiking out was a better option than sitting and waiting for the hillside to come down on top of them.

At noon on February 28, another group of 11 passengers and rail workers headed west, accompanied by conductor Joseph Pettit, who went to arrange delivery of supplies. Pettit promised to return and bring word to the remaining passengers about the safety of the hike.

It had warmed up overnight, and rain was falling as the hikers set out. Surprisingly, this time they found the trail somewhat manageable, and they reached Scenic quickly. However, Pettit, afraid he would not be able to get back to the train if he made the slide down to Scenic, hiked the cold, wet return to Wellington alone.

When he reached the train, he found the remaining passengers in a state of agitation. Throughout the afternoon, they watched as the rain caused the heavy snow to collapse hillsides all around them. Now they were terrified an avalanche would be their fate as well.

Upon his return, angry passengers set upon Pettit, demanding he move the trains into the tunnel or allow them to hike to Scenic where they would be safe.

The shortage of coal, however, made moving the train into the tunnel an impossibility, and Pettit felt hiking was still a dangerous proposition, especially for the women, children, and infirm on Local No. 25. Without Pettit's permission or approval, the passengers began to plan their escape at first light.

With the decision made, the dark mood immediately lifted. In her book *Northwest Disaster*, author Ruby El Hult, who interviewed many of the survivors of the Wellington avalanche disaster, tells of a lighthearted celebration that went on that night as passengers made plans to escape their nightmare and return to their real lives. There was singing and much laughter. The dark mood of impending doom lifted.

In the early hours of March 1, 1910, as the train passengers slept secure in the knowledge of their imminent escape from their precarious position, a thunderstorm rocked through the Cascade Mountains and lit up the tiny town of Wellington.

At 1:42 a.m., a lighting strike caused the snow on the hillside above the trains to let go.   The avalanche swept down the mountain and carried the passenger train, the Fast Mail Train, O'Neill's private car (with his secretary, Earl Longcoy, and his steward, Louis Walker, aboard), and two rotary snowplows into the Tye Creek ravine.

Rescuing Survivors/Finding the Dead
(March–July 1910)

The monstrous roar immediately woke the town of Wellington. People quickly rushed down the slope to the ruins of the trains and rotary plows, which were buried in debris, ice, and snow. As rescuers hunted for survivors, they had to dive into the wreckage headfirst, swimming in an ocean of snow.

There were survivors. Rescuers followed rivers of blood in the snow and pulled many people to safety in the wee hours of the morning on March 1, 1910. The three Grays, including 18-month-old Varden, emerged injured but alive. Raymond Starrett and his grandmother were rescued, while the whereabouts of the rest of their family remained unclear.

Others weren't so lucky. Rescuers found George Davis and his daughter, Thelma, lashed to a stump, dead. The entire Beck family perished. Conductor Pettit, Earl Longcoy, Louis Walker, and a number of the railroad workers on the mail car and rotary crews died.

Ida Starrett was the final survivor rescued. In her book, *Northwest Disaster*, Ruby El Hult tells Ida's story. The mother remained trapped for hours in the wreckage with her baby, Francis, struggling beneath her. For a long time she felt him wriggling, and in the moment his movement ceased, she knew he had died.

Ida also lost her father and her daughter, Lillian, that day, while her mother and oldest son survived.

When O'Neill returned from Scenic, it was to a scene of unspeakable horror. In spite of his battle, vigilantly fought against the storm, he had lost.

Ultimately, GNR counted 96 passengers and rail workers dead in the avalanche that took place in the early hours of March 1, 1910. There is some debate about that number. There were 96 bodies recovered, including 36 passengers and 60 railway workers. Six remain unidentified.

Estimates rise to as many as 113 dead. Many believe some bodies fell through the snow and ice and washed downriver, never to be found. This isn't as farfetched as it may sound as a number of undocumented laborers walked off of the job after their demands for higher wages weren't met. Since the laborers left in the chaos of fighting the storm, it was never determined who and how many had walked away.

The final body wasn't recovered until July. Wellington remains, to this day, the worst avalanche disaster in the history of the United States.

In the aftermath of the avalanche, everyone wanted to forget. The GNR quietly renamed Wellington as Tye in order to remove the town's association with disaster. Within 20 years, not only was there no trace of Wellington, but the town of Tye was gone, as well — a casualty of progress by GNR.

Part III: The Ghosts of Wellington

A Spark Ignited (February 21–22, 2009)

I am interviewing a team of local paranormal investigators, called Washington Anomalies Research (WAR) for an article in *Paranormal Underground* magazine. Tonight, they are taking me ghost hunting at one of Washington's hot spots, a mansion in Puyallup, Washington. It is to be my first crack at paranormal investigation, and I'm not sure what to expect.

I'm mostly agnostic when it comes to the belief in ghosts. I've had some experiences in my life that could have been paranormal, but the intervening years between what happened and now have blurred the edges of the incidents for me.

When I was in my 20s, I lived in a WWII-era apartment in the Navy town of Bremerton, Washington. Strange things happened there. Latched closet and cupboard doors opened and closed. The faucet would turn on with a creak and water ran into the sink, only to creak and stop a few moments later. At night in bed, I would hear footsteps, feel the bed depress, and hear someone whisper, "I love you," in my ear. With the whisper I could feel the wind flutter across my cheek, as if someone was whispering to me. We had a six-foot inflatable Godzilla that one day wound up in the middle of the bed with no explanation for how it got there. It freaked me out. I moved.

At the time, these experiences scared the heck out of me. Now, as a paranormal reporter, I'm not so sure what I experienced back then. It could have been paranormal, but there may be other explanations as well.

I've had a few other experiences since then, mostly in the past five years, and this has sparked my interest in finding answers. Still ... ghosts? I'm not so sure. There is no proof. I'd like to believe they exist, because for some reason the explanation of ghosts for the experiences I've had seems more palatable than the other options: either I am crazy or so susceptible to suggestion that I allow my imagination to run wild.

This is why I am here with WAR. I hope to experience something that sways me one way or another about the existence of ghosts.

I meet with the team at a nearby Shari's Restaurant for an interview before our trip to the mansion. There are six members of the team there, including the team's founder, David Martin.

As I interview them and record the answers into my trusty digital voice recorder (which will later double as a ghost-hunting device), I ask them to reveal the most impressive piece of paranormal evidence they have ever captured.

Three of them mention a photograph and an electronic voice phenomena (EVP) captured simultaneously at a place called Wellington. I've never heard of Wellington, but the place sounds interesting, so I make note of it.

After our interview, we head off to the mansion and spend a few hours there. In spite of a rather interesting potential EVP I capture on my voice recorder, and the fact that both of my digital still cameras died (permanently) at the mansion, I still don't really know about ghosts. I remain agnostic with no belief in one direction or another.

Even if I don't have the proof I was looking for, I have my story. I also have an excuse to buy a new and improved digital camera.

The next day, I e-mail WAR's other founder, Tracey Martin, who was not with us at the investigation. I ask about the picture and EVP obtained at Wellington, which she promptly sends me.

Looking at the picture and listening to the EVP, I know I have no choice but to visit Wellington. I don't know why, but suddenly I know the answers I seek with such intensity are there, waiting for me. Unfortunately, it is February. Wellington won't be free of snow until June. So, I will wait and go as soon as the snow clears.

WAR Experiences Wellington (October 2008)

The WAR team first investigated Wellington in fall 2008. The team's cofounders, David and Tracey Martin, are both self-proclaimed psychic mediums who anecdotally report they have been tested under controlled circumstances. There are others on the team who also claim to be sensitive, including Joe. I have had experiences with all three of them where it seemed their intuition was bang-on.

Each of the team's members has stories to tell about their experiences at Wellington. They have been investigating the location for approximately two years and firmly believe a number of spirits haunt it.

Today, nothing remains of the town of Wellington except for some slabs of building foundation and a half-mile-long crumbling concrete snow shed that the GNR built after the avalanche to protect trains running along the line.

There is no longer a train track running that high in the mountains. Instead, the GNR built a new track and tunnel at a lower elevation, near where the Scenic Hot Springs Resort once sat.

The former rail bed is now a hiking trail called the Iron Goat Trail. It runs along the route of the GNR, tracing the western slopes of the Cascades.

Where Wellington once sat is a trailhead. Traveling a quarter mile east from the parking lot along the Iron Goat Trail, you come to the abandoned Cascade Tunnel, which now remains closed due to the danger from collapse and flash flooding. Hiking about a quarter mile west from the parking lot, you come to the snow shed that protected trains from avalanches in the years between 1910 and 1929.

The snow shed is a behemoth. It is difficult to imagine what went into building such a massive structure in the days before the availability of automation and heavy construction equipment.

Nature is slowly reclaiming the mammoth structure. Animals dart in and out of the concrete giant, leaving behind their footprints in the soft dirt beside the trail. Leaves and trees form a canopy, blocking the open southern wall from direct sunlight.

The shed travels along a half mile of the Iron Goat Trail in a quiet and cool expanse before hikers continue in the sunshine to Windy Point. The western end of the snow shed is starting to collapse in a mismash of twisted rebar and concrete. The collapse wasn't the result of avalanches, as many suspect. Instead, the government tried to bring it down using dynamite nearly a half century ago, but the snow shed refused to fall.

About one-fourth mile down the snow shed sits an observation deck that looks out over Tye Creek and the site where the trains came to rest after the avalanche swept them down the mountain so many years ago. It is on this observation deck where WAR began to experience the   ghosts of Wellington.

Tracey and fellow WAR investigator Steve sat on the observation deck watching something rather odd on their first visit to Wellington. Although it was still partially daylight, a "cloud of black" came toward them from the opening in the snow shed that leads to the observation deck. The cloud then receded into the darkness of the shed once again.

On another visit, former WAR investigator Shane Bodiford set up his camera on a tripod on the observation deck as fellow investigator Joe conducted an EVP session. Shane was using slow exposures with the camera in order to capture images in the darkness, which was why the tripod was necessary. As Joe asked questions, Shane snapped a picture and then immediately noticed an anomaly on the screen.

In the picture, there is a giant, blue swirl of light rising above Joe's head (no small feat given that Joe is about 6'6") and his fellow investigator, Steve. At the bottom of the swirl, which sits slightly above the deck itself, there is what appears to be a doorway with what looks like a cuffed pant leg and an open boot stepping out of it.

At the same time Shane was taking the picture, Joe captured an EVP on his digital voice recorder.

"Are there any children present?" Joe asks on the recording. Following his question, there is a sudden snap, followed by a loud rumble. Distant voices sounding like they are coming from a number of people start to well up until a loud whisper whips out, "Avalanche! Get out!"

On another visit, former WAR investigator Greg Nichols sat on the observation deck when he began to hear voices coming from inside of the shed. Getting up to investigate, he found no one in the shed. He observed a light swinging back and forth at about waist height, much as a lantern would swing if it was being carried. He snapped three pictures, one after the other. The first picture shows nothing other than a dark snow shed. In the second picture, there is a round light about three feet off the ground, exactly where Greg saw the swaying light. In the third picture, there is once again only the dark snow shed.

Stories told by WAR investigators Steve, David, and Tracey are a little different. Steve frequently experiences equipment failure at Wellington. Whenever he is there, his cell phone shuts off and won't turn back on until he leaves.

David tells the story of a missing battery pack on his first visit to Wellington. Searching all through his camera bag, he was unable to locate it. When he returned home, however, he found the missing item. It was sitting neatly on top of the camera in the camera bag that he searched repeatedly while he was at Wellington.

Tracey's other experience at Wellington is one many women who travel through the snow shed apparently share. It involves an area that another team has coined as Area 61 because of a painted 61 marked on a snow shed support pole. According to Tracey, something stops her when she gets to that area, and it won't let her go on. She says it feels like a malevolent energy that is guarding something in the   area. Whenever she reaches Area

61, she is always turned away.

On more than one occasion at Wellington, members of WAR report hearing what can only be described as a party.

"There is music," Tracey says. "We hear voices. On one occasion we smelled malt liquor."

Since Wellington is very remote, it is highly unlikely any sounds from nearby civilization could be mistaken for a party. The nearest town is 30 miles away. The ski resort remains closed when the road to Wellington is passable. There is no electricity in the vicinity, and only a few winter ski cabins are located within several miles of Wellington.

What they have found in their investigations of Wellington has kept the WAR team coming back to Wellington.

"I believe Wellington is haunted," Tracey says. "For the most part, it has a good energy. There's just one thing that feels malevolent."

"We come here because it's a beautiful place," David says. "It's a peaceful place. If you're looking to experience paranormal activity, it's also a really good place to have an experience."

Joe adds, "Buckle your seatbelts, because you're in for quite a ride. If you are open to it, then Wellington is the place to experience ghosts."

The Pull of Wellington (May 25–July 10, 2009)

J im and I have been discussing getting up to Wellington. When a colleague contacts me to ask for a list of Washington's most haunted places, Wellington is the first place I mention.

Although I have yet to visit Wellington, I've spent the winter researching. The more I delve into the mystery of the place, the more I am convinced I need to visit as soon as is humanly possible. Already, Wellington is exerting its pull. For me, the ghost town has its own gravitational force. It is a tug I can no more resist than the force that holds my feet firmly tethered to the Earth.

Tracey e-mails me to let me know that the road to Wellington is finally clear. Now it's a matter of getting my schedule free to make the three-hour drive from my home to Stevens Pass. I'd like to go immediately, but it is the end of the school year and that involves all sorts of things like attending concerts, driving kids to and from camp, taking family vacations, and more. Wellington will have to wait.

Then there's the challenge of finding its location. I know it sits along the Iron Goat Trail, but the turnoff to the road isn't marked, and I don't particularly want to park at one of the marked trailheads and hike until I find the place. I will if I have to, but that's a last resort. First, I'll try and figure out exactly where it is.

After several false starts and busy weekends with the kids, I finally manage to schedule a spur-of-the-moment trip to Wellington for July 11. Jim and I will travel up and meet WAR, which kindly gives us directions on how to get there. Finally, I will be a satellite orbiting Wellington no longer. The gravitational pull it exerts is bringing me closer.

NWPIA Falls in Love With Wellington
(July 2004)

If one believes in fate, then it almost seems like providence brought paranormal investigators Bert and Jayme Coates to Wellington. Bert, who bears an uncanny resemblance to Superintendent James O'Neill, went hiking one sunny day in July along the Iron Goat Trail. The rest, as they say, is history. Little did he know that a sun-dappled hike would lead him and his wife, Jayme, to one of their greatest loves, Wellington.

After that initial hike, Bert got on the Internet and learned Wellington's history. It wasn't long before he and Jayme had their team, Northwest Paranormal Investigation Agency (NWPIA), driving up the mountain pass to investigate. What they found there has kept the team coming back several times every month throughout each spring, summer, and fall since July 2004.

To say Bert and Jayme love the ghosts at Wellington may be an understatement. Wellington is their passion. They feel loss during the winter months when the roads are impassable. In the spring, they make the 45-minute drive to Wellington frequently from their home in Gold Bar, Washington, to measure how high the snowpack is and then estimate when they can return to visit their friends once again.

Since their love affair with Wellington began, Bert and Jayme have made it their business to know everything about the town. They've studied its history extensively and traveled over every inch of terrain, including venturing down the steep slope to the site where the trains came to rest after the avalanche. There, a great deal of debris remains from the train, such as lanterns, parts of brakes, screens, and more.

Bert and Jayme also feel it is their job to protect Wellington. As more paranormal groups become aware of the activity there, they venture up to the peaceful location. NWPIA wants to make sure Wellington remains peaceful and pristine — both for the hikers who frequent the area and the ghosts that remain there. Because of this, they try to be there when they hear that teams are coming into the area. They act as tour guides, as well as preservers of the pristine nature of the site.

"If you do come to Wellington, please be respectful," Bert says. "It's a beautiful place, and we'd like to keep it that way."

They also caution that it is a wild place, replete with indigenous wildlife.

"We've seen bears," Bert says. "Once in the ravine, we had a cougar drop down on us."

Wildlife is part and parcel of nature, and Bert and Jayme are well aware that while in nature, one must be on guard. While they don't interfere with the wildlife at Wellington, both Bert and Jayme carry handguns to protect themselves, their team, and any visitors to the area from any threat of wildlife.

Bert, Jayme, and their team members at NWPIA have amassed an impressive array of evidence from their time spent at Wellington.

They are both thoroughly convinced it is haunted, and Bert and Jayme aren't people who are quick to jump to that conclusion. They weigh all evidence carefully, always looking for alternative explanations. Wellington, however, often defies explanation.

While NWPIA's experiences are too numerous to count over the past five years, there are some that stand out as being significant, two of which they captured on video. The first is what they believe to be the ghost child of Wellington.

One evening during a routine investigation, Bert was filming as they walked down the snow shed after dark when something popped out from behind a pillar. In the video, a small white image in the shape of a child peeks out from behind one of the snow shed's support poles and then pops back behind it.

The team has analyzed the footage thoroughly, and they can't come up with an explanation for the anomaly.

In another video captured in October 2008, viewers can hear the voice of a very young child calling out, "Mama."

At the same time they captured the voice on film, the investigators heard the child call out. No children were present at the time.

It is for these reasons many of the members of NWPIA have come to believe that one of the spirits that remains at Wellington is a child. For more evidence of a child spirit, they look to reports by a number of their team members who experience touches on their legs, as if someone child-sized is running past very quickly, as well as EVPs captured of children's voices.

Another common phenomenon reported by NWPIA is the party. Like WAR, the NWPIA investigators frequently hear music, talking, and "people generally having a good time," according to Bert.

Jayme says, "We hear a banjo. We hear an accordion."

According to both Jayme and Bert, the party starts up many summer evenings at about 9 p.m.

Members of NWPIA have come up with ways to identify some of the many entities they feel are present at Wellington. One regular character out of many is the one they call "No Face."

According to Bert, No Face seems to linger in the first quarter of the snow shed, just before the observation deck. He has made himself present to investigators from the team, including Jayme. Whenever someone spots him, No Face shows up as a full-body apparition with a white blur where his face should be.

Jayme had a run-in with No Face this past September. "He didn't have a face," Jayme says. "It was like a face — white, cloudy — but no eyeballs."

In the same area of the snow shed, other investigators on the team have seen black shadow figures in the shape of human beings. In one case, an investigator saw two at the same time — one leaning up against the north wall of the snow shed with his arms folded and another stepping out from the wall.

While they have no name for the apparition that hangs out in Area 61, they are well aware of his presence. They see him in the form of a black shadow that flits from pole to pole at superhuman speeds.

Jayme has had a very personal run-in with the Area 61 apparition.

"It was weird," Jayme says. "I had been thinking just a few weeks before and wondering what it would be like to have an apparition go right through me. Would I really experience its entire life and all of its thoughts and feelings when it did? I decided I totally wanted to have that experience."

One night shortly after making that decision, Jayme and another investigator were sitting down in Area 61 watching the black entity flit from pole to pole. Jayme squatted down to look at the figure when it charged straight at her.

"In that moment," Jayme says, "I decided I wasn't ready."

She quickly jumped back and shone her flashlight directly at the charging shadow, and it dissipated right before her eyes.

Jayme is firmly convinced that at least some of the entities that hang out in the snow shed are men.

"There were a lot of single men up here," she says. "It doesn't surprise me they respond to women."

In fact, in one of the team's many EVPs that they've captured over the years, a male voice responds to Jayme with a rather personal comment.

"Okay, last chance to come out and say hello," Jayme says on the recording.

Just then, a scratchy male voice is heard saying, "I want to see you naked."

In another EVP, which is on the team's Website, Bert and Jayme are investigating when a soft male voice very clearly tells Bert, "Leave her alone."

These are just a few of the experiences NWPIA has amassed in their five years of regular Wellington investigations. They've collected a number of EVPs and some interesting photographs. Some of the EVPs are startlingly clear, although there is a not quite human quality to the voices. In many, there is indication of intelligent interaction.

In one EVP, a female investigator says, "We're not here to hurt you."

A clear voice responds, "Don't believe you."

In another, a male investigator asks, "Hello, is there anybody here?"

The response comes in a child's voice. "Yes. There are."

"It's an amazing place," Bert says. "One year we captured an EVP — we lost it, but I can still remember it. It says, 'Oh look, the scientists are here.' That EVP made me feel good. Not because we are scientists, but because the ghosts here seem to recognize what it is we are attempting to do, and are responding to it."

Jayme says, "When I first came to Wellington, I was afraid of everything. I was afraid of the dark. I was afraid of ghosts. Now, I'm just not so scared anymore."

Our First Visit (July 11–12, 2009)

Finally, the day has come for me to visit Wellington. Jim and I park the kids overnight with friends. Then we invite a colleague, Mike, to join us. We get directions from Tracey before making the trip.

My husband Jim and I have lots of equipment with us: cameras, high-definition and normal-definition recorders, video cameras, EMF detectors, and, of course, flashlights with all kinds of lighting schemes like colored lights, black lights, and infrared. Jim's a gadget guy. While he remains quite skeptical about the existence of ghosts, he most definitely can't resist a good gadget. In this way, he's perfect for paranormal investigation.

The drive takes about 3 ½ hours, but it is a gorgeous day and a beautiful trip through vineyards, river valleys, and small towns that climb into the mountains along Highway 2.

As we take the turnoff from the highway and begin the 800-foot drop from the summit down into Wellington, I can feel its gravity drawing me nearer.

Daylight lasts until about 10 p.m. in Western Washington this time of year, so it is still bright when we arrive in the parking lot at about 7 p.m. Sunlight streams through the trees and bounces off the peaks that surround the area where the tiny town of Wellington once sat.

It is very quiet. Occasional sounds of large trucks filter down from Highway 2, which sits across the valley and above Wellington. For the most part, all we hear are the quiet, peaceful sounds of nature and a slight breeze ruffling the leaves of the trees.

The parking lot is wide enough to hold two rows of perpendicularly parked cars with room in between for a wide two-way roadway. A two-stall outhouse sits on the south side of the lot with a trail extending past it to the east and west. The tall trees behind the outhouse hide the fact that just a few yards beyond their edge is a precipitous drop down the slope into the valley. A field of long grass scattered with a few trees sits to the north of the parking lot. Behind it bubbles a small creek on the banks of which once sat the Bailets Hotel.

Tracey greets us in the parking lot and leads us west along a well-maintained gravel trail. The path is mostly flat with a minimal grade that meanders slightly downward as we head west through tall trees. Off to our right sits the rusted-out carcass of an avalanche canon. About ¼-mile down the trail, there is a wooden bridge, and beyond it a giant concrete structure.

As we approach the snow shed, we hear the sound of rushing water. It is so loud as it bounces off the cement structure it stops all conversation as we troop across the bridge and into the snow shed.

Although I've read about the snow shed in my research, nothing has prepared me for its massive scale. It soars nearly 20 feet above my head, lined with gigantic concrete support pillars. The north side of the shed is a solid wall. The south side consists of two rows of the pillars, and the sunlight leaks through the heavy foliage that nearly obscures it.

It is shadowy and cool in the snow shed. Outside, it is probably 85 degrees, but once inside the shed the temperature drops at least 15 degrees. As we walk, I notice how sounds bounce up and down the concrete structure; however, they carry only so far before they die away. Within just a few yards, the sound of the rushing water that seemed so overwhelming has completely dissipated.

Immediately on entering the snow shed, there is a nearly oppressive heaviness in the air. All of us notice it.

I am about to comment on it when Mike says, "Does it feel really heavy in here?"

Tracey tells us that it is a frequent occurrence at Wellington. History weighs heavily here, and you can't help but be aware that something serious has transpired. The heaviness isn't always there, Tracey says, but frequently.

David meets us partway down the snow shed and leads us to the observation deck. We sit down on the two benches to soak in the atmosphere. Almost immediately, I feel someone poking me in the shoulder. Thinking that it is an errant plant poking through the rails of the observation deck, I turn around to look. No plant, animal, or person is there.

As I sit on the bench, the random pokes continue in different spots along my back and shoulders. This is the same bench Joe and Steve sat on when Shane captured his photograph and Joe captured the EVP.

Tracey, who is sitting on the bench across from me, pauses mid-sentence and says, "Someone just pulled my hair."

She goes on to explain it felt as if someone had taken a single strand of hair and deliberately pulled it out of her ponytail. I get up and look to see if her hair is caught on anything. It isn't. It seems the spirits at Wellington are active and ready to interact with us.

"Who keeps poking me?" I ask.

On my recorder a soft feminine voice that we don't hear at the time pipes in. "Just me."

After experiencing the fifth or sixth poke, I jokingly suggest any entity present pokes Mike, who is very afraid of ghosts.

Later, when reviewing audio from our visit, a whispered voice says, "No."

After some time on the observation deck, Jim, Mike, and I decide we want to continue east and see the rest of the snow shed. Tracey's 13-year-old son, Bobby, leads the way. Tracey and David stay back at the observation deck. As we leave, Tracey tells me to pay attention to what I experience and tell her about it when I return.

At first, all I notice is the oppressive heaviness of the air. Then, small things begin to happen. I am overcome by the sudden onset of chills. Mike becomes inexplicably itchy, which lasts for about a minute before disappearing as quickly as it came. The hair stands up on my arms and on the back of my neck, and just as I am about to say something, Mike says the hair is standing up on his arms and neck. It is nothing concrete. Instead, there are just small, odd sensations as we move down the snow shed.

As I'm walking along chatting with Bobby, one minute everything is fine and pleasant, and in the next moment, I am gobsmacked. Without warning, I am dizzy and nauseated. My heart is pumping and every fiber of my being screams at me to stop and not go on. The anxiety is horrible and quite unlike anything I've ever experienced before. Although I've never had one, I am certain this is what a panic attack must feel like.

I tell Jim, Bobby, and Mike what I am experiencing, and then I take a look around me as I try to catch my breath. I notice a long "bridge" running along the ground and a pole with a 61 painted on it, graffiti-style. I wait a few moments for the anxiety to recede, but it stays inside of me, pounding and intense. It is as if everything inside of me is screaming, "GET OUT" at the top of its lungs. Still, I came for the experience, and I am determined to go forward.

Warily, I place one foot on the bridge. My feet feel like lead, my legs feel like Silly Putty, and my innards are an odd combination of fire and Jell-O. Attempting to take a deep breath into my clenched lungs, I slowly put one foot in front of the other as I walk across the bridge. About 30 feet from the start of the bridge, the physical sensations subside just as quickly as they came. Now, the end of the snow shed is in sight with the sunlight streaming through it. The relief is overwhelming. And then I notice something else, as well. The heaviness I've felt since I entered the snow shed is completely gone.

When we exit out the west end of the snow shed onto the grassy trail, the temperature immediately jumps by 20 degrees. The scenery is breathtaking. We pause along the trail to read some of the historical markers, and Bobby and I chat about inconsequential things.

Later, when reviewing the high-definition and regular audio recorders I carry with me, I hear a high-pitched, almost child-like voice say — over both my voice and Bobby's voice — "Mmmmm hmmmm, Bobby. Hi."

Bobby and I are the only two with high-pitched voices: Jim and Mike both have relatively deep voices. The voice on the recording speaks clearly on top of both of us. No one hears anything at the time.

After hiking another 100 yards or so down the trail toward Windy Point, we decide to head back. Once again in the snow shed, as we approach the long bridge by the pole marked 61, the anxiety and physical symptoms pile on me. It is almost unbearable in its intensity. This time I don't pause — I just keep walking in spite of my pounding heart, and about 30 feet from the pole everything returns to normal.

Tracey is waiting at the overlook, and she asks what experiences I had as I walked down the snow shed. When I describe my sensations at the bridge, a knowing look crosses her face. The same thing happens to her in the exact same location.

Twilight is approaching now, and we resume our seats on the observation deck benches to await the arrival of NWPIA. Occasionally, as we chat, someone jumps and says that they have been touched. I am sitting on the forward edge of my bench, resting my elbows on my knees. As I talk to Tracey, who sits on the other bench, I sense that someone has managed to take a seat on the bench behind me without my noticing. I can hear breathing in my ear just off my left shoulder, and I feel the presence right behind me. I quickly turn around to see who sat down next to me. No one is there.

In spite of knowing no one is behind me, the sensation persists. As the twilight turns to dark, I can still feel the presence behind me. It follows me with small, choppy footsteps wherever I go. It is as if a small, persistent child remains with me for the rest of the evening. Every time I turn to look to see who is behind me, there is no one there.

When it is nearly dark, we all make the quarter-mile walk back up to the parking lot. NWPIA has arrived. Tracey introduces me to Bert, whom I immediately begin to pump for information about Wellington.

As I talk with Bert, Jayme arranges for a group to head down into the ravine to conduct an EVP session at the crash site. Her group forms and heads off, and then we return to the snow shed.

While there are still some lingering traces of residual light outside of the snow shed, inside it is another story. It is pitch black. We traverse the bridge, clear of the noise from the stream, and I still hear those tiny footsteps following close behind me. Occasionally, I feel a brush on my thigh as if a tiny body bumps up against it.

Just as I am about to say something to everyone about my small visitor, Tracey does her psychic medium thing, claiming, "We have somebody with us. They're curious about what we are doing."

David shines his flashlight beam down the snow shed, and something fast and shadowy flits across in front of it at about eye level 50 feet in front of us.

"Did you see that?" we all say in unison.

"Turn off the flashlights," Tracey says. "Let's do an EVP session."

As soon as the flashlights go off, the snow shed is immersed in the blackest black I have ever experienced. There is absolutely no ambient light. I feel a brush against my leg as Tracey begins to ask questions.

In the middle of the EVP session, Tracy says, "David?" and turns on her flashlight.

"I thought David was standing right to my left," she explains.

He isn't. He's standing about 10 yards ahead of us in the snow shed focused away from us — staring into the black further down. There is no one within 10 feet of Tracey.

It is only later I learn that the place where we stopped is what is commonly referred to as "the child pole," because it is where NWPIA captured the video of a childlike shadow peeking out from behind the snow shed support.

We turn on our flashlights and continue down the snow shed, past the observation deck. As we approach what I now know to be Area 61, I am once again stopped cold by the same overwhelming anxiety. Tracey halts at almost the same moment I do and says she won't go any farther. David stands and watches down the bridge, where we all see a large, black mass speeding from pole to pole. Knowing that wild animals are a real possibility, I keep my fingers crossed it is a ghost. If it is an animal, it is a tall one, and it's really, really fast.

We return to the observation deck with my little friend still following me closely and occasionally bumping into my leg. I know he is there. I can hear him, feel him, and sense him as if someone is several inches inside of my personal space bubble.

Bert has set up a laptop computer and projector to show images of 1910 Wellington onto the north wall of the snow shed. He plugs both into a power inverter. He explains this is one of the things that they do to increase activity and that the ghosts there typically seem to respond to it. He tells us of an evening when they decided to try asking about Superintendent James O'Neill.

"The place went crazy," he says. "All of a sudden there were shadows and noises everywhere."

On the observation deck, we watch the slide show and talk with Bert for a few more moments, and then Mike, Jim, and I head up the trail for home. We have a long drive ahead of us, and it is getting late. Plus, I'm pretty sure Mike is scared, since he's the one really pushing to get home.

As I walk away, I notice a picture of James O'Neill projected onto the snow shed wall. Just then, the inverter emits a high-pitched, unceasing wail. We walk back to Bert to see what is going on.

"Have you tried this before?" I ask.

Bert answers in the affirmative.

"So this is the first time that the inverter has behaved this way?"

"Yes."

Jim, who is an electronics guy, takes a look at the inverter and says it is attempting to die. Bert turns it off, unplugs everything, and then plugs it in again. The wailing continues, so he unplugs everything again and leaves it turned off.

We head back down the snow shed again toward the parking lot.

It's quiet in the car. Mike and Jim gab in the front seat while I sit in the back, reflecting on my experiences. My little friend from the snow shed is still with me. He hasn't left my side, and I get the sense it is a young boy. He rides along with me for a while. If I listen closely, I can almost hear him talking to me. As Mike and Jim continue to talk in the front seat, I very quietly tell the child he can't come with us and that he needs to return to Wellington. As soon as I say it, I am alone in the back seat.

Later, Jim and I are all tucked into bed when I feel my little friend back in the room with me. I can hear him shuffling around. I can feel his presence, which is now familiar to me since he followed me all evening. There is a soft thunk in the room.

"You can't stay here," I tell him. "You'll scare my kids."

Just like that, he is gone.

The next day, I talk with Tracey and tell her about my visitor in the car.

"I think something came with me in the car last night," I tell her, knowing how crazy it sounds.

Instead of responding with horror at my obvious insanity, Tracey's response surprises me. "Really," she says. "Tell me about it."

I tell her about feeling the child with me all evening, as well as in the car on the way home and then later in my bedroom.

"That's interesting," Tracey says, "because we had something in the car with us when we left, too. We had to pull over to the side of the road so that David   could tell it to leave."

Tracey and David left a few hours after we did. Is it possible that my friend from the car returned to Wellington, only to hop in the car with Tracey, David, and Bobby?

After recovering from my grogginess left over from my late night, I eagerly review the hours of recorded evidence from Wellington. Much to my surprise, there are a number of anomalies on both the high- and low-definition recorders. In some cases, I can rule out a sound captured on the low-definition recorder (an Olympus) when I hear it on the high-definition one (a Zoom H4 recorder). In other cases, I can't come up with explanations.

The "No" in response to the request to poke Mike is on the Olympus, but not the H4.

"Mmmmm hmmmm, Bobby. Hi," is on both.

"It's me, just me," is on the Olympus recorder only.

Along with those, I've captured several other potential EVPs on the Olympus. Most are whispers or very quiet voices that aren't easy to discern. A few seem to be in response to direct questions.

Now, I am curious to learn more about the story of Wellington. I jump on Amazon.com and order *The White Cascade* by Gary Krist, which tells the in-depth story of the Wellington disaster.

After experiencing Wellington first-hand and reviewing all of the evidence, I am eager to return. While the evidence is interesting, I don't feel it is conclusive, so I want to get back as soon as possible to see what else I can   capture.

Still, I know after my first experience at Wellington, I am closer to being convinced ghosts exist than ever before. Even Mr. Skeptic himself, Jim, seems less sure of his disbeliever position than before.

"If any place could get me to believe in ghosts," he tells me, "it just may be Wellington."

I feel exactly the same way.

Hearing the Spirits of Wellington
(Summer 2007)

It was the summer of 2007 when EVP expert Medea Aguiar-Light first visited Wellington. Since then, she has returned repeatedly. Medea is the perfect EVP expert. Her hearing is phenomenal. She can pick out sounds with her bare ears that I can't even hear on headphones jacked up to max volume.

"I just have really good hearing, and I know what to listen for," Medea says. "I listen for consonant sounds, which allows me to make out what is being said."

Medea has an extensive collection of EVPs she has captured at Wellington. It seems the spirits there have always been more than willing to talk with her.

While having good ears may account for some of Medea's luck capturing EVPs, does it account for all of it? When we first met, I asked Medea if maybe the spirits of Wellington talked to her for more reasons than that she had good ears. Could it be that she was clairaudient?

While at first reluctant to admit that clairaudience might come into play, as well as good hearing, Medea finally realized there was a decent chance that was exactly what was happening. How else could she explain that she could hear what most others couldn't, and usually have it backed up on recordings?

"I think I may be a psychic medium," Medea says. "It's a hard one for me to admit because it flies in the face of what I have believed in the past, but it seems a likely explanation."

In the past few years since Medea has been visiting Wellington, she has talked extensively with the spirits there. Her manner as she goes about communicating is intense but compassionate. She makes sure the spirits know she cares about them, she will keep coming back to visit, and while she is there, she will try very hard to hear what it is they are saying.

As she talks with the spirits, her tone is conversational and her questions are thoughtful and intelligent. Many times she pauses and says things like, "I think I can hear you. Can you come closer?"

After each question, she tells you if she has "received" an answer and expresses her hope the answers that she hears with her ears are on her recorder.

"Sometimes it's frustrating for me and for the spirits," Medea says. "I can hear them well enough to know they are talking, but I can't always make out what they are saying."

More than once, Medea has captured spirit voices on EVP expressing frustration with the fact she doesn't always hear exactly what they are saying. Still, she keeps trying. As a result, she has collected an impressive array of EVPs. The spirits at Wellington seem eager to communicate with Medea, apparently knowing she is their best bet of getting the message across.

While the sheer volume of Medea's EVPs from Wellington is remarkable, the content makes them amazing. When we met at Wellington for the first time in August, Media had her computer and some headphones with her so she could allow me to hear the EVPs she had already described to me on the telephone.

"I've collected all of these EVPs in the past few years," Medea tells me.

The first EVP she has me listen to is of a very clear voice that sounds like a young boy. Medea explains that during the EVP session, she mentioned aloud she kept hearing a female voice. She then heard (and captured on recorder) a voice that said, "I'm not a wady. I's a boy."

Another recording captured at Wellington has a very young child's voice saying, "It's you mommy, sleep."

On another recording, Medea asks, "Are you a child?" and a voice quickly replies, "Yes."

One evening while alone in the parking lot, Medea lit a small kerosene burner to make a cup of coffee when she captured the same child's voice saying, "Put it out!" very clearly as soon as the flame flared up. When she allows me to listen to the EVP, even I can hear the voice.

Medea has also come to believe there is a child spirit up at Wellington. Along with EVPs, she has also had the experience of feeling as if a spirit child is in the car with her, as well as at home with her.

According to Medea, it started with an EVP of a young child saying, "Are you a nice lady? Because I'm a good boy to leave."

The next time she was at Wellington, Medea told the boy he could come with her, but only if he promised not to frighten her children.

She tells the story of driving home from Wellington with her husband, Mike, when they both began hearing a murmuring voice in the back seat. Convinced one of her voice recorders had somehow turned itself on, she searched the car for it. It wasn't a voice recorder. It was then that Medea became convinced that the boy was taking her up on her offer to come home with her.

According to Medea, this was the first of several home visits she received from the child.

"He never stays long," she says. "I don't think he can. Something keeps pulling him back here."

The child isn't the only spirit that Medea has heard more than once at Wellington.

"There's a man with a Midwestern accent," she says. "Clearly, he has a sense of humor."

One night while sitting on the observation deck with a group of investigators, they asked any spirits present make themselves known by knocking. From underneath the decking came two crisp knocks.

When they asked the spirit to knock again, Medea captured a man's voice with a Midwestern accent saying, "No more parlor tricks."

On other recordings, Medea has captured the same voice arguing with another male voice and calling him a "slack jaw," which was a term in common usage at the time that Wellington was in its heyday.

While many investigators concentrate on the snow shed, Medea believes that the parking lot is just as active. It is there where she can sit quietly and listen.

One night while making a cup of coffee, Medea offered to pour a mug for any spirits who were present. On her recorder, she captured several voices.

"Thank you for putting me a cuppa coffee," a woman's voice says.

"Thank you," another voice says.

"A whole cuppa hot coffee just for me," says a gruff man's voice.

Sometimes, the spirits are more forthcoming than others. Occasionally, they will even share their name with Medea. In one EVP, she asks a spirit's name and is told "Brasca." In another, the spirits reply in whispery voices, "My name is Jason. My name is Jeremy."

Medea has also captured singing in the parking lot. She has a clear recording of a woman singing as if she is humming to herself as she goes about her business.

It is rare that Medea doesn't capture EVPs when she is at Wellington. While not all are extremely clear, many are. The voices from that she captures on her recorder sound like people going about their daily lives and attempting to communicate with all who wish to listen.

A Small Visitor (July 15, 2009)

I t has been a few days since my first visit to Wellington, and I am still absorbing it. My son, Tanner, is at a friend's house, Jim is at work, and I am sitting alone in my living room working.

Earlier today, the UPS man delivered *The White Cascade*, and I am looking forward to reading it and gaining deeper insight into the tragedy at Wellington.

My dogs calmly curl up next to me on the couch, when all of a sudden there is a loud click on the marble floor in the entryway. The dogs go crazy.

I get up to see what made the noise and try to quiet the dogs. I look around but don't see anything. Suddenly, I have in my head the image of a young boy. He is about three years old and is wearing knickers; heavy, black wool socks; and a heavy pea coat. On his head is a newsboy cap.

The dogs stand facing the stairs and bark at nothing. Finally, I quiet them and look outside the screen door to see if something outside could have made the noise.

From behind me on the stairs a soft, childlike voice says, "Hi."

The dogs start barking again. I whirl around, but there is no one there. Then I see what made the click that originally brought me into the entryway. My son Tanner's saxophone strap had been sitting on the stairs underneath a pile of his books. I know it was there, because he put it there just an hour ago, anchored by heavy books so that the dogs wouldn't drag it off.

Now it is lying in the middle of the entryway, and I know it wasn't there a few minutes ago when I went through the foyer to do laundry. The plastic clip that attaches to the saxophone must have made the click on the marble floor just moments before. I pick it up and drop it. It clicks softly. I pick it up again and throw it on the floor with force. This time, it matches the sound I heard.

The dogs have been with me the whole time since I last passed through the foyer. Not only that, but they are small dogs. Tiny dogs who lack the strength to drag the strap out from under the heavy books on the stairs. They range in size from four to about 15 pounds.

Mystified and just a little freaked out, I return to the living room. The image of the boy remains in my head, and I have a sense of small footsteps following behind me.

I reach for *The White Cascade*. I turn to the back of the book and find a list of the dead. I'm looking for a three-year-old boy.

There aren't any I can find at first. Then I see a listing, Beck, unknown first name (child). This is the only possible three-year-old boy in the bunch. I dig through the pages of the book and discover a passage that talks about "the three-year-old Beck boy" playing with a toy train with another child on the train. He goes on to mention that the boy is fascinated with his toy train.

I get on the Internet and start digging to see if I can find the child's name. On a Web page dedicated to online cemeteries (who knew there was such a thing), I find photographs of the graves of the entire Beck family. His name is Leonard. Judging by the birth date on the grave, he was just short of three when the avalanche occurred.

Next, I look on the Internet to see if I can discover what kids wore back in the winter of 1910. In all of the catalog images, I find dark knickers; heavy, woolen black stockings; lace-up black boots that rise to about ankle height (more like high-top shoes, really); wool pea coats; and newsboy caps. It's exactly the image I have been seeing in my head.

Could Leonard be the boy I am seeing in my head? Perhaps more importantly, could this be the boy who followed me all around Wellington and then followed me home?

My head is thrumming with the possibilities, but at the same time, I'm pretty certain I am crazy or over-imaginative. It makes no sense I keep seeing this child in my mind.

Then I start to think about everything. In my travels until now, I haven't come across anything talking about the kids on their train or their names or ages. I had no idea that there was a three-year-old boy on the train or whether there were any children on the train at all. Not only that, but when I felt like the child was in the car with me coming home from Wellington, there was a moment when we were running parallel with a train across the flats and it felt as if the energy in the car was extremely excited. There, in the book in black and white, it talks about the boy's fascination with a toy train. Next, there's the clothing. I'd visualized it down to specific details in my head before I saw the 1910 winter clothing on the Internet.

Maybe — just maybe — I'm not crazy.

A Visitor From the Past (March 3, 2007)

Several times each year, Carolyn Rehor and her husband travel across Stevens Pass from their home in Stanwood, Washington, to their cabin on the Wenatchee River. They make the drive so often, in fact, it has become routine.

The route takes the Rehors through scenic vistas, past flowing rivers, and up into the heart of the mountains where they drive right past the turn-off to Wellington.

Carolyn is in her early 60s and was born in Washington, where she has lived all of her life. Like many in the state, she'd never heard of Wellington or what happened there. It's easy to drive across Stevens Pass and see only scenic vistas. Even if you look carefully, all you'll see is a swatch of parking lot or a peek of snow shed poking out from behind the trees.

Wellington has been gone for so long, it has disappeared from the collective consciousness of the citizens of the Pacific Northwest. With the exception of history and railroad buffs, and those who live in small railroad towns like Skykomish, Washington, many are unaware of the role the GNR played in the history and development of Washington State.

On the afternoon of March 3, 2007, the Rehors drove home across the pass to Stanwood. It was raining cats and dogs, as it so often does on the western slopes of the Cascades.

Shortly after driving over the summit of the pass at about 3,600 feet elevation, Carolyn noticed a strange sight outside her car window. There, along the side of the road on the non-freeway side of the concrete barrier, stood a man. Carolyn described him as over six feet tall and extremely well muscled.

He was standing in the incredible downpour wearing what appeared to Carolyn to be old-fashioned railroad clothes, an engineer's cap, and a headlamp. Especially odd was that he wasn't wearing a coat despite the freezing mix of rain and sleet that was coming down in a deluge. She thought the man might be hitchhiking, because his arm appeared to be raised. If he was, it was in what she termed "a very odd location" where he was barely visible to passing traffic and in a spot where cars couldn't stop to pick him up easily.

"He had on a railroad cap and one of those lights," Carolyn said, referring to his headlamp. "It wasn't a helmet with a lamp — it was a hat. At first I thought he might be a miner, but later I realized that there is no mining in the area. Plus, it was just really strange that he wasn't wearing a coat given the weather."

Carolyn continued, "I stared at him, and he stared at me. He followed my eyes with his eyes — or at least he followed me with his head. I couldn't see his eyes or make out any facial features except for the shape of his chin. As we passed him, I turned my head to continue to look at him. He did the same thing. He turned his head to look at me. It was so clear!"

When she got home, Carolyn started researching the area and learned of the Wellington avalanche disaster.

"After that, I assumed he was associated with the railroad disaster," she said.

Although Carolyn has never seen anything similar again, she says, "Now I know why he was there and why it was March. I still look for him."

The Kids Make New Friends (July 25, 2009)

Since he heard about our experiences at Wellington a few weeks ago, Tanner has been asking us to take him there. Today, we are headed to Wellington with Tanner, his stepbrother Kevin, and his two friends, Matthew and Mackenzie, in tow. We have decided to stay only during daylight hours — just to give the kids a flavor of Wellington. I don't know if they are quite ready for Wellington after dark.

Because Wellington is a hiking trail, I'm not terribly worried about taking them there for a day hike and to hang out for a bit.

The kids are all equipped with various digital voice recorders, cameras, video cameras, EMF detectors, and more. We have also come with toys to see if we can entice the children of Wellington to play. In my black Safeway grocery sack, I've got a stuffed dog, a jump rope, some jacks, a rubber ball, and a battery-operated wooden Brio toy Thomas the Tank Engine train with a circle of track. We also have with us the full complement of paranormal investigation paraphernalia, which Jim refers to as "The Paranormal Box o' Fun."

We arrive at Wellington at about 1 p.m. It is another stunning day, with brilliant sunshine and a soft breeze. There is only one car in the parking lot besides ours, and I see a couple walking up the trail. The man is batting bugs away from his head. He looks familiar, and I realize it is Bert and Jayme who are walking toward us.

We stop and talk with them for a few minutes. Bert tells us that they have been up on top of the snow shed. I tell him that the kids are hoping to experience some activity.

Bert says, "Oh wonderful! They love kids."

Needless to say, the kids are excited to hear this. They are equipped and ready to go. Each is holding a recorder. Two also have cameras, while the other two have EMF detectors. Despite the fact it is early afternoon, they are also all ready for dark, with headlamps and cap clips affixed to various parts of their clothing.

I have my recorder, as well. It is hanging from a lanyard around my neck. As soon as we hit the trail, Tanner turns on his recorder. In the very first seconds that the recorder runs, you can hear a high-pitched voice chattering over his. It is impossible to tell what the voice is saying, but it has a definite speech pattern, and it isn't anything that we are aware of or hearing in the moment. Maybe Bert is right, and the ghosts at Wellington will respond to the kids as they apparently did to Bobby on our previous visit.

First, we hike all the way to the end of the snow shed, with a quick stop on the observation deck. The snow shed feels heavy from the moment we enter it. Almost immediately, Tanner and Matthew insist that something keeps touching them on the legs.

As the kids walk through the snow shed, they keep up a steady stream of questions. Not for Jim and me, but for the ghosts. As they ask the questions, they wave their recorders around.

When we approach the bridge at Area 61, I feel the familiar anxiety taking over. Mackenzie mentions she feels funny and is getting a headache. Jim says he is nauseated. We walk quickly across the bridge, and everyone's symptoms clear up as we approach the end of the snow shed.

It's quiet at Wellington today, and aside from running into Bert and Jayme, we don't encounter a soul. We head back into the snow shed and then plan to go sit on the observation deck.

While we are sitting on the deck, Mackenzie feels someone pat her on her head. Next, she starts to see odd disturbances in her field of vision.

We decide to get toys for the children to set up on the observation deck and see what happens. On the way out, the kids walk well ahead of us. When we get to the bridge at the entry to the snow shed, Jim stops and walks around it.

"What are you doing?" I ask him.

"I'm trying to see if this bridge is made of old railroad ties," he says.

Just then on my recording, a really high-pitched voice that sounds very young says, "This is not your bridge."

Jim and I are the only two there. The kids are already 200 feet down the trail, and no one is in the snow shed to the west. I have the directional microphone of the Zoom H4 pointed at Jim as he talks.

After feeding the herd, we grab the bag of toys and head back down to the overlook with the equipment in tow. Jim sets up the circle of track, and Matthew places his recorder in the center of it. We place the train in the middle of the observation deck with a video camera pointed at it, and Jim turns it on. We all return to our seats and watch silently.

After a few minutes of the train running, on Matthew's recorder you can hear shallow breathing as if coming from an excited child.

Bored with watching the train go round and round, Matthew, Mackenzie, and Tanner ask if we can go back to the "scary bridge." We decide to leave Jim and Kevin with the toys, and the four of us walk down the snow shed.

On the video recording of the observation deck, the train falls off its track. On Jim's recorder, you can hear a small, childlike whimper. On camera, Kevin sets the train back up and turns it on again. It circles the track a few more times before falling off again. Jim instructs Kevin to go ahead and leave it off. As soon as Jim says "off," Jim's recorder captures the same childlike whimper.

After turning off the train, Kevin and Jim sit in silence. On Jim's recorder, you can hear a high, wispy voice humming the first bar to "Mary Had a Little Lamb."

Meanwhile, Tanner, Matthew, Mackenzie, and I are back at the Area 61 bridge. I'm feeling my characteristic anxiety.,Tanner and Matthew, who are standing side by side, both jump simultaneously and say, "Something just touched my leg!"

"Who touched the boys' legs?" I call out.

Just then, we all hear a high-pitched giggle. On review of the evidence later, the laugh shows up both on video camera and digital voice recorders.

We leave Area 61 and head to the collapsed end of the snow shed. About 50 feet from the Area 61 bridge, I suddenly feel as if someone is behind me.

"Take my picture," I tell Tanner.

He snaps a few photographs behind me. On later review of the photo, an interesting luminous figure shows up about 50 yards behind me in the snow shed. Review of photos snapped in succession show the figure only in the one picture.

We return to the observation deck and pack up. The kids are on full-court press to stay after dark, but dark is still several hours away.

Finally, we decide to drive into Leavenworth for dinner and return at dusk. We tell the kids we don't plan to stay much more than a few minutes after dark.

As I say this, a voice shows up on my voice recorder that says, "You stay too long."

As we are walking out of the snow shed, Tanner jumps, feeling as if he's been touched again. On the digital voice recorder, you can hear him say, "Whoa!"   followed by a faint, high-pitched voice that either says, "I'll try" or "Nice try!"

When we return after dinner, it is nearing dusk. There is still no one there. We have the place to ourselves.

Matthew decides he wants to try out our talker box. The talker box is a box that has an EMF chip and an allophone chip. The theory behind it is that spirits can learn to manipulate the EMF in order to cause the allophones to form words. I've never used mine before, but I've seen other teams have some success with them.

Matthew turns on the talker box, and he turns on a digital voice recorder as well. We head down to Area 61. Already, it is quite dim in the snow shed, and the kids are getting a taste of just how dark Wellington can be.

An idea pops into my head. Maybe whatever is in Area 61 is the spirit of one of the unnamed Italian laborers killed in the avalanche, which is why he seems so darn ticked off all of the time.

"Are you Italian?" Tanner asks.

The talker box responds. "Not Italian."

As full-on darkness nears, we tell the kids it is time to head home. There is great wailing and gnashing of teeth. We return to our car and begin the three-hour drive home. For the first 10 minutes, the kids put on headphones and listen to their recordings to see what they got. Quickly, the mind-numbing boredom of reviewing evidence sets in, however, and   they hand their recorders to me.

A Chilling Encounter (August 2006)

John and Jeanne White are history buffs. They especially love the history of the railroad and GNR. It was this mutual love of history that led them to visit the historical town of Wellington on a sunny day in August 2006.

John was intimately familiar with the story of the Wellington avalanche. He'd read Gary Krist's book, *The White Cascade*, as well as other historical accounts of the 1910 avalanche.

His daughter even recalls him telling her stories about the avalanche.

"I remember that he told me about a mother who laid buried by snow on top of her baby as it smothered to death," she says.

John and Jeanne hiked around the trail for a while, and then John decided what he really wanted to do was go down and see the wreckage site for himself. Jeanne didn't think she was physically up to the steep walls of the ravine, so she said she would wait for John while he looked around down below.

As John hiked, Jeanne seated herself outside of the snow shed near the trailhead down which John had just disappeared. The area where Jeanne sat was open and provided excellent visibility in all directions. She could see if anyone was coming.

After she sat for a while, Jeanne noticed something that caught her by surprise. A person was standing there, not making a sound.

Assuming it was John, she looked up and was startled to see it was a young man dressed in turn-of-the-century winter clothing. He looked at Jeanne and then turned and silently walked down the same trail to the ravine John had taken.

As Jeanne sat and contemplated the oddity of the young man's clothing, especially given the warmth of the sunny day, John popped out from the trailhead.

"Did you see that young man?" Jeanne asked. "He was dressed so strangely."

John gave Jeanne an odd look.

"What young man?" he asked. "There was nobody there. I was by myself on the trail and down in the ravine."

As the couple walked back up the snow shed, Jeanne thought about what she had seen. What could it be?

We'll see his car in the parking lot, she thought.

When they reached the parking lot, there was no other vehicle beside their own, as had been the case the entire time they were there.

Jeanne remains baffled by her experience at Wellington. Her daughter, who is a paranormal investigator, is not.

"I know what she saw," she says. "It was one of the ghosts of Wellington."

A Return Trip (August 17, 2009)

I t is another beautiful, sunny afternoon. The kids have been pestering us to take them back to Wellington and allow them to stay after dark. Finally, we relent. We'll go and stay just an hour after dark. It's not as if the kids have to twist my arm to visit Wellington. Every time I leave, I can't wait to return. It is as if it calls to me when I am not there.

We get a later start today, and we pack a picnic for dinner.

We arrive at Wellington in the late afternoon. There is one other car in the parking lot. A young, earthy-looking couple are poking around the parking lot area. We gather our gear and immediately head down to the snow shed. The kids are all business this time, walking quietly and paying attention to every little thing.

When we enter the snow shed, it has an entirely different feel than before. It feels peaceful and serene, like a mountain hiking trail and not a spooky haunted place. Perhaps my familiarity with the place has changed my perception, or maybe it is my budding migraine. Suddenly, I get that familiar tingling along the side of my face and goose bumps on my arms. I call it my "spidey sense," and it seems to indicate the presence of some kind of an entity.

Matthew and I are lagging about 50 feet behind everyone else. Just as my spidey sense goes off, the TriField EMF meter he is carrying goes crazy. It spikes all of the way to the top and then seems to pulse in a series of lessening spikes.

Some paranormal investigators feel ghosts have high electromagnetic frequency (EMF), which they can measure on an EMF detector. There is no science supporting this, even though it is a popular "ghost hunting" tool. Many non-paranormal things can set off EMF detectors, including moving too quickly, cell phones, battery powered equipment, and electrical circuitry.

We stand still for a few minutes and just watch the needle on the meter jump around. This is interesting, given there are absolutely no electrical currents running anywhere within a few miles of Wellington. I know because I've taken baseline readings more than once on the same meter. Matthew and I mark the pole with a stick and head down to the observation deck with everyone else. Everyone's cell phones are supposed to be turned off, but that interference could cause EMF spikes.

Mackenzie and I sit together on the bench. Tanner and Matthew sit across from us. Jim and Kevin run back to the car to get a piece of equipment we have forgotten.

As Mackenzie and I sit side-by-side, we both keep feeling as if something is bumping the bench and making it shake. At the same time, there is also a subtle rolling of the deck under our feet.

We look at each other, startled. "Did you feel that?" we ask, nearly simultaneously.

Mackenzie notes that she is having the same type of visual disturbances that she experienced the last time we were on the observation deck at Wellington.

Jim returns to the overlook with Bert and Jayme in tow. Bert proceeds to tell me about the active Friday night with black shadows, whispers, and more. It all seemed to center around one small area in the snow shed.

We leave the observation deck and lead Bert and Jayme to the pole Matthew and I marked earlier where we were experiencing EMF anomalies.

"Yeah — this is where it was," Jayme confirms.

The pole where I'd had a "spidey sense hit" and we had an EMF spike followed by several surges of EMF energy is exactly where NWPIA's Friday activity occurred.

Bert and Jayme walk back up the trail. Jim, Matthew, and Mackenzie decide to go check out the debris field, while I stay behind with Tanner and Kevin. As they work their way down the ravine, the three of us head to Area 61. I have it in my mind to speak a little Italian and play some music with Italian lyrics on my iPhone. I haven't totally given up on my theory yet that whatever hangs out in Area 61 is an angry Italian laborer.

As we approach Area 61, the air seems to weigh a ton. The old physical sensations are back.

Just as we get there, Tanner calls out in an anxious voice, "It's here!" He stares down the trail, almost in a trance.

My walkie talkie beeps and breaks the trance. Jim and the kids are headed back up the trail. We go to meet them. As we walk, a voice whispers in my ear.

I keep asking, "What?" but I can never quite make out what it is saying.

So far, things have been just a little intense, so we take the kids back up to the parking lot where they can eat their dinner and work out their sillies.

After dinner, the kids are in high spirits. They are goofing off. I turn my recorder on and dictate into it.

"It's after dinner and the children are in high spirits," I say.

Ahead of me, I watch them running, jumping, and laughing.

On my recorder, a tiny, high-pitched voice very clearly says, "Want to play?"

"Okay," I tell the kids. "Get it out now. When we hit the snow shed, it's over!"

On my recorder, the same voice (and also the same voice who said, it "wasn't a bridge") responds, "What are you talking about?"

Our first order of business once we hit the snow shed is to set up an infrared, motion-activated game camera in the area by the pole Matthew and I marked earlier. We hope if there is activity and motion in the area when we aren't there, it will be captured on the camera.

Next, we go sit on the observation deck for a few minutes. As I am sitting there, I feel someone stroke the back of my neck. Almost immediately afterward, someone strokes the top of Mackenzie's hair repeatedly as if petting her. Then Matthew jumps.

"Whoa!" he says. "Something just poked the back of my head. Hard."

Now it's Tanner's turn. He and Mackenzie are sitting side-by-side on a bench, and they both jump at the same time. Something has stroked their legs.

As dark rapidly approaches, we sit quietly. Then, we start to hear noises in the snow shed. We go inside to investigate. It is pitch black.

Our natural inclination is to head toward Area 61. We're ready this time with all kinds of stimulus. We learned some Italian in the car on the way here. Matthew and Mackenzie brought train whistles. I've learned how to say, "It's cold" and "It's snowing" in Italian.

Jim walks behind us, filming on our video camera. He's got two infrared lights with the camera. Both lights and the camera are all on separate power supplies. As soon as we hit Area 61, all three shut off simultaneously, despite the different power supplies and mechanical on/off switches one has to slide and click into the on or off position. When Jim looks, the switches have slid from the on to the off position. At the exact same time, the Zoom H4 digital recorder I am carrying also shuts off. For a moment, Jim can't get his equipment to turn back on. Then, as if nothing happened, they turn back on and Jim resumes filming.

The kids blow the train whistle and I call out, "*Fa freddo!*" (It's cold!)

The kids blow the train whistle again, and I call out, "*Nevica!*" (It's snowing.)

We turn on the music with Italian lyrics. After the music plays for a moment, Matthew jumps sky high. Something has placed its hand firmly on his back and given him a rough shove.

I turn off the music, and Jim calls out Latin mass. Now, it's Tanner's turn to jump as something grabs his leg in a firm grasp.

We linger in Area 61 for just a moment longer, and then, calling out, "*Ciao!*" and "*Grazie!*" we head back up the snow shed. As we are leaving, something firmly grasps the back of my arm. I turn to tell the kids to not grab me, and there is no one behind me. All of the kids are on the other side of me, and Jim is 15 feet behind us filming.

When we get to the observation deck, we notice two of the digital voice recorders are dead, despite the fact I put in fresh batteries earlier in the morning. The video camera (with a fully charged battery) Kevin is carrying has also completely drained.

As we leave, I feel my little friend, who I've come to believe is Leonard, is with me. I talk softly to him as we walk up the trail. We pack up and get in the car. I can feel Leonard still with us in the car.

From the back seat, Tanner says, "He's here, isn't he, Mom?"

"I think so," I tell him.

Strange things are happening in the car as we drive. The video screens in the back seat blink in and out. My cell phone keeps making weird noises. Tanner's iPod shuts on and off repeatedly.

"Leonard," I say. "You're making things stop working in the car. Maybe you should go home and visit a little later."

Then he is gone. All of the equipment returns to normal function. The rest of the drive home is uneventful.

As we head toward home, I look at Jim, the skeptic.

"So," I ask. "Do you believe Wellington is haunted?"

Without hesitation he answers, "Yeah. I do."

Tuning in to Paranormal Activity
(October 2008)

Steve Johnston has been investigating with WAR for quite some time. What's interesting about Steve is that he doesn't experience the paranormal in the same way that many do.

"I really think it is because I am autistic," Steve says in his characteristic soft-spoken and introspective manner. "I think that really opens me up."

Steve has a form of high-functioning autism known as Asperger Syndrome. At 23, he is bright, talented, and ambitious. When you talk to him, unless you know that he has Asperger Syndrome, he doesn't seem like he has any form of autism. He just seems shy. Shy but friendly.

I've investigated with Steve before, and I'm familiar with his style. He's a gadget guy. He likes to fiddle with gadgets. At the same time, if there is something there, he is the first to feel it and sense it. On our previous investigation together, for instance, Steve spent the night in a hotel room dreaming of a woman screaming in his face. During our investigation the next night, I captured an EVP of someone screaming in the same room.

Wellington tends to mess with Steve's head.

"I'm not really sure what it is," he admits. "There are just certain spots where some kind of feeling comes over me, and I have to Scooby-Doo."

I asked, so it's only natural that you would.

Steve explains that Scooby-Dooing is what happens when his body reacts without conscious thought. His legs get moving, and he runs as fast as he can without really going anywhere. It continues until he realizes he is doing it.

There is one particular place at Wellington that really gets to Steve and causes him to Scooby-Doo. It's Area 61.

"I'm not sure if I'm picking up on something that's there or if I am picking up on Tracey's feelings," he admits. "All I know is that something happens and my feet are moving as fast as they can."

It's worse when Steve is tired.

"I hate it when I get tired," he says. "That's when ghosts really mess with me. It opens me up even more, and I can't control it."

Steve isn't really aware when he Scooby-Doos. Afterward, he has virtually no memory of it. It seems to be an automatic response brought about by what just might be paranormal activity.

Filming a Documentary (August 26–27, 2009)

W e've decided to film a documentary about
Wellington. I don't know a lot about making
movies, but Steve is a film student, so he can help
us. After all, I think, making a documentary is just another way of
telling a story, and I am a storyteller. I have confidence that, with
the love I've developed for Wellington, I will be able to tell its
story well. Not only that, but filming a documentary gives me a
great excuse to be up there as often as I possibly can in the weeks
and months to come.

Jim and I will provide all of the funding and most of the
equipment, with the exception of a few borrowed cameras. We
will produce. I will direct, write, and edit. Jim and Steve will
film. Mike is trying to become an actor, and he asks if he can host
the documentary. While I'm not quite certain how we will tell the
story with a host, we agree that Mike can be part of the film as
one of the producers, as well as onscreen. If the hosting doesn't
fit with the story, then Mike can at least provide narration. He has
a great speaking voice. We arrange for him to meet us at
Wellington, and Mike connects beforehand with everyone else
who will be there that day.

Jim, Mike, and I arrive at Wellington at about noon and meet Bert
and Jayme of NWPIA, Tracey and David of WAR, and Tony and
Jackie Scappini of Left Coast Paranormal. There are also a few
paranormal groups up having a look-see after an article about

Wellington appeared in this weekend's *Everett Herald*.

I have a schedule for each of the cameras for the day. One camera will record interviews, while the other will capture B-roll around the site. We head off to set up a camera at the opening of the Old Cascade Tunnel, which serves as a backdrop for the on-camera interviews. We spend most of the remaining daylight filming background, interviews, and B-roll around the site as we wait for darkness to settle in.

It's crowded up at Wellington today, but we manage to stay away from most of the other visitors.

At dusk, we gather into two groups and head into the snow shed. I am with David, Steve, and Mike. Jim films us. David also has a camera.

The five of us move toward Area 61, which has been its own malevolent self all day long. As we walk, David tells me something has followed us all the way down the snow shed. It is a curious entity, he says. We can hear it moving around off to our left. David borrows my audio recorder and moves to where we hear the movement.

"Who are you?" he asks. "How old are you?"

On the recording, a soft voice answers, "Sixteen."

Looking down toward Area 61, we see a familiar dark figure flitting back and forth between poles.

As we approach, I notice that Steve is standing and staring off into the distance.

"Steve," I call out. "Steve!"

He doesn't seem to hear me. He just stands and stares.

After a long time in the same position, he gives a jerk and shakes his head.

"What happened?" I ask.

"What do you mean?"

"You just stood there, staring," I tell him.

He says he doesn't remember. "I must have zoned out."

I turn to ask Jim if he got it on film, and then turn back to Steve. He's staring off into the distance again. He doesn't move — not even a muscle.

"Hey Steve, are you okay buddy?" Mike asks, noticing his odd posture.

"He's zoned out," I tell him, using Steve's terminology.

Suddenly, moving like a marionette, Steve's entire body jerks as if pulled by a string, and he starts walking in the direction of Area 61. Only his legs move. The rest of him — his upper body, his head, his face — remain as still as a slab of marble. It is one of the strangest things I have ever seen.

Then, the string jerks again, and Steve whips around to walk rapidly in the other direction, still moving nothing but his legs.

Once again, the string jerks and he heads toward Area 61 again like a zombie. We've stopped following and all just stand watching.

As suddenly as it began, it is over, and Steve is Steve again.

"What the hell was that, Dude?" Mike asks.

Steve looks confused.

I explain to him what happened. He shakes his head. He has no recollection of the last few moments.

We return to the observation deck to meet up with the other team. They report a few voices in the snow shed but not a whole lot of activity. After regrouping, Jim, Steve, and David decide to take a walk back to Area 61. I stay on the observation deck. I'm pretty sure I've had enough of Area 61 and its bad self for one night.

After about 15 minutes, they return.

"How is it?" I ask.

"All quiet," David says. He goes on to explain it is as if nothing had ever happened there. The energy has totally changed.

"We want you to come with us," Steve says.

"To Area 61?"

"Yeah," he tells me. "We have a theory."

"And just what is that?" I ask.

"We think it responds to women."

Great.

Still, in the name of exploration (and good video), I get out of the comfy cocoon I have created for myself with a blanket and apprehensively follow Steve and David to Area 61 with Jim filming.

It's as if I am walking through the park on a bright sunny day. For the first time ever, I feel nothing in Area 61 — or anywhere in the snow shed. All is quiet. We turn to go back to the observation deck.

We run into Jayme and Jacque, who suggest everyone go sit on the observation deck for a little bit.

"Sometimes when it's like this, we go hang out in the parking lot or on the observation deck," Jayme explains. "Usually after a while, the activity starts up again."

We take her suggestion, and all of us gather on the observation deck. We sit wrapped in blankets staring at the stars.

The stars in the mountains are incredible on a clear night. With no ambient light, it feels as if you can see every star in the universe. We begin to share our stories of the paranormal, just a bunch of kids sitting around on a campout trying to spook one another with scary stories.

From inside the snow shed   comes a noise. And then another.

And another. Tony and Bert go to investigate. It seems as if the activity is picking up once again.

We split into groups. I'm with Bert and Steve, and we're headed east in the direction of the child pole. Jacque, Tony, and Mike decide to go west to Area 61. Everyone else remains on the observation deck.

As Bert, Steve, and I walk, we start to see black shadows coming out of the north wall of the snow shed. At the same time, we hear voices that sound like they are coming from the direction of the parking lot.

Suddenly, there is a rustling in the bushes off to my right. It's not a ghost kind of rustling, but an extremely loud, wild animal type of rustling. Bert shines his light, but nothing is there.

I sniff the air. Something isn't quite right. I turn to Bert.

"I smell cat pee," I say.

Bert stops for a moment. "Yeah, so do I," he says.

"Huh," I say. "Weird."

The three of us continue to watch the shadows for another minute, and then it dawns on Bert and me at the same time.

"Wait!" I tell him as we exchange a look. "Cat pee — that isn't good."

"Nope," he says. "Let's head back to the observation deck."

We're pretty sure a cougar is stalking us, or at least there is one very nearby. Once we are on the observation deck, Bert contacts the other group on the walkie talkie and tells them to come back, as well.

I am sitting on my customary bench as I watch the other group gather at the head of the boardwalk that leads to the observation deck. All around them the bushes are rustling, and the odor of cat urine is very strong. Suddenly, there is a huge "thunk" underneath the boards of the observation deck. The group at the end jumps, and Tony draws his pistol.

It looks like we're done for the night, just when things were starting to get good. On the way out, we walk in a tight pack with those of us who are armed on each side.

It is the first time I've ever fled from a cougar, and I can't help but think, I don't have to be the fastest person here. I just have to be faster than one other person.

On the way, we stop and pick up the game camera we set up without turning it off. The motion sensor in the camera snaps bits of film as we race up the snow shed and to the safety of our cars in the parking lot.

An Odd Anomaly (September 13–14, 2009)

It's our second day of filming. Since a cougar cut us short last time, we hope to get more investigation filmed during this visit.

We arrive at noon and spend the day filming interviews and B-roll. I am at the Cascade Tunnel with Steve conducting interviews, while Jim is off with other members of the crew filming the site.

Jim and I have been to Wellington a few times during the past few weeks for additional filming with Jayme and Bert. We've also been to Cascade Station and Windy Point to obtain additional footage.

Our time here has been wonderful. It's been a sunny, warm summer, and Wellington is the perfect place to spend time with friends and family. During our past few visits, we haven't been looking for evidence, so I'm eager for tonight's investigation.

This time we have a few more people with us. Medea has joined us, as have two NWPIA members, Tim Corr and Paul Barber. Joe from WAR with us, as well as Shane and Greg of Ghost Hunters of Washington are also here. Of course, Tracey, David, Steve, Bert, Jayme, Jacque, Tony, and Mike have all returned.

Another paranormal team is here, as well. They've heard about Wellington and have come to check it out themselves. They ask if they can investigate with us, and we tell them they can. Their names are Scott and Derrick, and they are with a new paranormal group in Marysville, Washington.

The day of filming goes well and is relatively without incident, except for one thing. As Steve, Tim, and I walk back down the trail toward the parking lot from the Cascade Tunnel, I capture what has to be one of the oddest audio anomalies I've ever encountered.

My recorder is in my front pants pocket with the microphone peeking out of the top. Tim and I chat as we walk down the trail. Other than the sound of our voices and footsteps, all is quiet.

Then, over the top of my voice, another voice rings out, sounding as if whoever is making the noise has their lips right up against the microphone in my front jeans pocket.

"Whoop!" it says, playfully. "Whoop ... whoooooooooop ... whoop ... whoop."

The three of us continue walking and talking, oblivious at the time to what is being recorded. Next, comes what sounds like a child cocking a toy gun. "Click, click — pkew!"

Finally, after another few seconds, the same voice laughs. All told, the recording lasts a good minute and none of us hear a thing. I discover the oddities only later when reviewing my audio files.

As dusk approaches, we gather and split up into a couple of groups. The first group containing Medea, Steve, and various assorted members of both   teams — heads to the observation deck. They plan to search from the observation deck west toward Area 61.

Our group consists of Tracey, David, Bert, Jayme, Jim, Derek, Scott, and me. We are going to work from the observation deck back toward the parking lot.

We stop for a moment on the bridge before entering the snow shed. Jayme and I discuss a walking stick.

In the middle of the conversation on my recorder, you hear a voice interrupt our conversation.

"What's a walking stick?" it asks.

As soon as we enter the snow shed, Tracey says there is a man who she believes to be "No Face" with us. She describes his clothing and height, and Bert recognizes him as No Face.

As we move on, No Face follows at a distance. Next, Tracey stops near the "child pole." At the same time, we both exclaim that our "spidey sense" has gone off.

As we work our way toward the overlook, Tracey and David both tell us that we are attracting a crowd. According to them, we have two children, No Face, and several other unnamed spirits with us.

We move onto the observation deck and take a seat. The spirits, it seems, are talking to Tracey. First they tell her through images that they had a Teddy bear, they miss it, and they want a new one. Hopefully, that's the kids. Next, Bert asks what they need to do to get the adults to trust them.

"It feels to me like the town," Tracey says. She goes on to explain that while a tragedy happened there, many people from the town remain there now out of love for the lives they built there. While they are happy there are monuments to the dead in the disaster, they want to be remembered too because their town was once there, and then after the disaster it just quietly faded away.

As we are sitting there, my voice recorder captures a raspy male voice saying, "Hi there!"

Just after the voice, I jump because something has grabbed my heel from beneath the bench. Jayme and I shine our lights under the bench, but there's nothing there.

We see the other team move past the observation deck toward the parking lot, and we decide to go into the snow shed to visit Area 61. Tracey is understandably apprehensive. She has never ventured beyond the start of the bridge because of the clear signals that she receives telling her not to.

As we reach the end of the observation deck boardwalk, Tracey tells Jayme that a male figure has stepped eagerly toward her. He tells her his name is Sergei.

Later in the parking lot, when Jayme tells Medea of the encounter with Sergei, Medea asks, "Sergei or Sergio?"

On her recording, an accented male voice is heard saying, "Sergei."

As we move down toward Area 61, Tracey's apprehension increases. She says walking   toward it is like swimming through a thick fog. She can barely see, so she clings to the back of David's shirt.

Ahead of us, we see a dark shadow flitting back and forth, as it always does. As we reach Area 61, my recorder captures what can only be described as a growling, angry voice saying loudly, "You suck." It is my favorite Wellington EVP ever.

When we get to the bridge at Area 61, Tracey stops and asks the entity there why he is so angry and aggressive.

After listening for a moment, she says, "He protects them."

"Protects who?" she asks, speaking to the entity. And then she jumps, visibly startled.

"I wish I could put a microphone on the inside of my brain right now," she says.

"What's he saying?" I ask.

"He's shouting, 'YOU SHOULD KNOW.'"

Just then, the video camera captures the sound of four sharp footsteps that sound like hard-heeled boots walking on wood. No one is moving, so the footsteps aren't coming from one of us.

After a pause, Jayme asks if we can cross the bridge. "If you don't want us to come across," she says, "you need to make a noise to let us know."

We hear nothing and cautiously start to proceed across. For the first time ever, Tracey has crossed the threshold of Area 61, and she's not enjoying it very much.

I, too, am feeling that same old feeling, but I'm used to pushing through it.

As we walk in a single file across the bridge, David calls out, "If you want us to stop, you need to let us know."

Just then, a loud and resounding thunk comes from behind us on the bridge. We all jump and whip around.

Sheepishly, Jim says, "Oops, it's just me. I fell off of the bridge."

We all pause and allow our hearts to stop trying to thump their way out of our chests, and then we decide to return to the parking lot and re-form new teams. As I walk up the snow shed, I talk to Bert about my concerns about the children at Wellington. Bert tells me that while compassion is good, I shouldn't take on the kind of responsibility I seem to be accepting for the children there.

Jim is walking ahead of us, filming Bert and me over his shoulder. As we reach the child pole, on the video you can see something white and cloudy quickly streak across in front of Bert and me at about waist height. One second, there is nothing there. Then, there is a white, cloudy blur. And then it is gone.

In the parking lot, we meet up with the other investigators and share what we've experienced. The other group says that they saw the usual figures in Area 61, and Medea captured a voice on recorder saying, "It's the Grim Reaper," in response to her question, "Who's there?"

While in the parking lot, I capture a recording of someone singing.

After a while, Medea, Tim, Jim, Steve, Mike, and I decide to head down to the observation deck while the snow shed is clear of people. Jim, Tim, and Steve stand at the end of the boardwalk, while Medea, Mike, and I conduct an EVP session on the observation deck.

During the EVP session, Medea starts asking the children questions. Interestingly, as she hears an answer, the same answer pops into my head. As we compare notes, we discover they are the same.

It seems two children may be present and answering our questions. One is a girl, and the other is a young boy. It appears we may have two of the Beck children with us.

Medea tells them we worry about them and asks if their mom and dad are with them. The answer is no, but they tell us there is a man who takes care of them. Occasionally, one of the three of us hears sounds like laughs or voices nearby. At one point, I feel a touch on my leg, and a moment later, Medea is touched on her leg in exactly the same place.

Medea asks if one of the kids will run by really fast and touch Mike on the hand.

Just then, the air on the observation deck changes. I am overwhelmed by nausea, and Medea is feeling it too.

She hears the man say to Mike, "If you want to see kids, go home and see yours."

As Medea and I continue to attempt to talk to the kids, she captures an EVP of an adult male voice saying, "Y'all don't care about us."

When she asks the kids if the man who takes care of them is nice or the boss of them, and the kids answer, "The boss," she captures an EVP of the same man saying, "Ain't seen anybody beatin' on you."

Medea hears male voices at the end of the boardwalk, but no one is there.

As the man who has joined us becomes more aggressive, the atmosphere of the observation deck changes from peaceful to malevolent. We notice Jim, Tim, and Steve are no longer at the end of the observation deck. They have disappeared somewhere in the snow shed to parts unknown. Little do we know that, at the same time we are talking with the man, Steve has "zoned out" again and Jim is following him in the direction of Area 61 with a camera.

"Somebody's here, and he's pissed," Steve says on video right before he completely zones out. This time, Steve's zone-out lasts for four to five minutes, and he doesn't remember any of it.

On the observation deck, I ask the angry man who has joined us to please knock on the wood of the deck if he wants us to leave.

There is a knock on the   wood.

"Was that you?" I ask. "Could you please do that again so that we know it is you?"

There is another knock. Message received.

We gather up our things and start to walk down the boardwalk to the parking lot. Just then, on my recorder I capture a voice saying, "Go away."

As we walk down the boardwalk, Medea keeps trying to explain what it is she was experiencing with the angry man, but as she tries to speak, she feels him poke her and growl, "NO!" in a loud, angry voice.

That's it. Medea is done for the night.

We meet back up with Jim, Tim, and Steve and walk up the snow shed together, each sharing our tales of what had happened while we were split into two groups.

When we reach the parking lot, it is well past 1 a.m., and we're ready to call it a night. I am so exhausted and emotionally rattled that I feel as if I don't care if I ever see Wellington again.

After packing up our equipment, we head out for the night.

Believing in Ghosts (July 11–September 25, 2009)

My husband, Jim, is certainly not one to believe in ghosts. Or at least he hasn't been up until now. He is an uber-science geek with a background in nuclear engineering, if that tells you anything.

When he first agreed to go to Wellington with me, he went out of an interest in history and a love of hiking in the mountains. He didn't really care much that ghosts might be there. Instead, he put up with the ghost thing in an effort to support his wife.

Wellington wasn't Jim's first investigation with me. He went to one other, spending a weekend in a rickety and freezing cold hotel as various paranormal groups from the state ghost hunted. Nothing happened on that ghost hunt that made him change his mind about the existence of ghosts.

Jim knows all of the stories about the experiences I've had. While he has never come right out and told me I was deluded, he always has alternative explanations for everything I've experienced. Sleep paralysis. Active imagination. Faulty wiring. If it was anomalous, there was a logical explanation for it.

I think that's why he wasn't prepared for Wellington. Of course, neither was I. From our first visit there, he began to experience a philosophical shift from "no way" to "could be" to "maybe" to "probably." I don't know if he's gotten all of the way to definitely yet, but it is a pretty tough leap to make, even for me.

When I asked Jim what started the shift in philosophy, he told me that it started on our very first visit there.

"I know you, and I trust you," he tells me. "And I saw you react in some pretty psychologically interesting ways to things. I know you well enough to know that you weren't making those things up."

With each successive visit to Wellington, Jim became a little more convinced. What finally got him, however, was the total simultaneous equipment failure that we experienced on our second trip to Wellington with the kids.

What began as an interest in history has become something far more personal to Jim. Like me, he has come to love it, and he is intrigued by what he has experienced at Wellington.

The Child Pole (September 25, 2009)

Two days later, we are back at Wellington. My exhaustion quickly gave way to an eagerness to return.

Jim and I have driven up to Wellington today with toys for the children. I wasn't able to get a Teddy bear, but I have a stuffed animal and a ball.

It is another beautiful day. On the way in, we notice how quickly fall has come to Wellington. The trees have all started changing to brilliant reds and oranges.

Jim and I take pictures of the crumbled foundation of the Bailets Hotel as we wait for Bert and Jayme to arrive.

When they get there, we grab the toys and take them to the child pole. We leave them there and hike to Windy Point. It is a gorgeous hike, the company is good, and the weather is perfect. It's sunny and not too warm.

On the way back, as we walk through the snow shed in the fading light, the shadows are already long as they slant through the trees. We hear a child's voice call out as we near the child pole. Bert, Jayme, and I all hear it. Somehow, Jim doesn't.

We have hiked all of the way from Windy Point, and we know no one is on the trail behind us. There is no one in the snow shed in either direction. When we get to the parking lot, there are no cars.

Could the voice have been one of the children of Wellington, thanking us for the toys?

Summer's End (October 24, 2009)

The time has come. It is my last visit to Wellington this year unless something miraculous happens with the weather. School has started, and Tanner is busy. I am not free to roam around, especially on the weekends, because he has soccer games on Saturdays continuing until mid-November.

Already I am feeling a sense of loss, but I am determined to enjoy my last visit to Wellington before the snow sets in.

We are having a party tonight. The party is to honor Wellington and thank the spirits there for the generosity they have shown in sharing their home with us.

Everyone who has participated in the filming of the documentary is there, and several of us have invited guests, as well. Mackenzie and Matthew have joined Tanner, and their parents Larry and Leslie have joined me.

My friend, Alli, is also there. She's been hearing about Wellington for months now, and she is interested to see what the flap is all about.

Tanner and I are the first to arrive. I am shocked at the changes in the past month. All the foliage is gone. Now the snow shed is exposed on the south side, and you can see all the way down to the creek.

It is cold and damp, but Wellington is still beautiful. Without all of its green finery, the beauty is starker and more haunting.

I have arrived a few minutes early for a reason. I finally found a Teddy bear, and it is in my bag waiting for delivery. Tanner and I walk down the snow shed, and I pause at the child pole, gently placing the Teddy bear in back, where it won't be trampled by the partygoers. I brought it for Leonard and any of the other children at Wellington. I hope they will have it to keep them company throughout the long winter months to come.

Tanner and I walk all the way down the snow shed. It has a different feeling today, even Area 61. It is quiet, and yet the quiet seems anticipatory. It feels to me as if something very special is about to happen.

I have no equipment with me this time. No cameras or recorders. This time I have come as just me to celebrate the ghosts of Wellington and to bid them farewell for the winter.

Silently, I talk to the ghosts as I walk through the snow shed, thanking them for all that they have given me. After all, I now know something that I didn't before. I know I have a soul that will survive death. There is great comfort in knowing that, and I owe the comfort to my friends at Wellington.

I feel as if my fear has been transformed. I feel like a new woman who can face the challenges the world throws at me, knowing there are those whose souls survived the worst and yet they still persevered. Knowing this, I know I can, too.

118

Tanner and I walk back up to the parking lot. Mike has arrived with his friend, and my friend Alli has arrived as well. We take them on a tour of the site, all the way from the Cascade Tunnel to the western end of the snow shed. When we return to the parking lot, even more people have arrived.

The skies open up, and the rain pours on us for a few minutes. Then it clears and a few stars peek through the clouds. Wellington grows dark early, ready to reveal its secrets to those who will listen.

Larry, Leslie, Matthew, and Mackenzie arrive. Larry and Leslie have heard much of Wellington from me and from their children, but this is their first visit. We set off in a group with Alli in tow to show them Wellington.

As we enter the snow shed, we meet up with Mike, Bert, and Mike's friend, who are on their way out. They've been hearing voices and seeing shadows down in Area 61, and Mike's friend is pretty excited. It's his first encounter with a ghost.

The snow shed is pitch black. For some reason, we decide to honor the blackness and walk without our flashlights. I walk ahead with the kids while Larry and Leslie walk behind us. Leslie keeps hearing the sound of small, choppy, quick footsteps behind her, and has to fight the urge to reach behind her to grab a child's hand.

Once, she hears a voice yell in her head, "Turn on the light!"

She complies, and her light goes on just in time to stop Larry from pitching head first into a little, dry streambed that runs across the snow shed.

Area 61 is quiet, but expectant. As we walk through, I feel someone off to my left, just behind my shoulder. They brush against me. As I turn to speak to whoever it is, I see there is no one there.

We walk all of the way down the snow shed and then back up toward the observation deck. The bridges in the snow shed are lined with candles, and the flames dance off of the walls. On the observation deck, a thin layer of frost has coated all of the wood, making it slick and treacherous. Winter is on its way.

Leslie still feels her small friend accompanying her as we walk back to the parking lot where a large bonfire is roaring. We join the party and warm up.

A few hours later, Mike and I decide to walk down the snow shed together. When we get to the observation deck, we encounter members of NWPIA who are goofing off taking "ghost" pictures using lighting effects and slow exposure. We stop to have our ghost picture taken, and then continue down to Area 61. The air still feels expectant.

We aren't talking much. My mind flashes back to a trip through the snow shed that I took with the kids earlier in the summer. When we stopped in Area 61, I talked to whoever was there.

"I understand why you are angry," I told him. "Nobody remembers you. Nobody remembers your sacrifice."

I am convinced the entity in Area 61 is one of the immigrant laborers who toiled to keep the trains free of snow and the tracks clear of ice and debris, only to receive poor treatment from the passengers and railroad alike before being swept to his death in an avalanche. He may not be Italian, as I previously thought, but I am certain he is a railroad employee.

I don't know how I know this. I just do. I've come to trust there are things I just know, and I no longer need to dig for an explanation. That is something else that Wellington has done for me.

That day with the kids, I made a promise to my friend in Area 61.

"I am going to tell your story," I told him. "I am going to make sure you aren't forgotten."

In the present, Mike and I walk to the end of the snow shed and turn around. As we approach Area 61, the atmosphere no longer feels expectant. Now it feels welcoming. It feels as if whatever is there is smiling at me.

As I step onto the bridge of Area 61, a chill runs through my entire body, my skin erupts in goose bumps, and the hair stands up on my arms. I look ahead and freeze in my tracks. There, standing in the middle of the bridge is a tall dark figure. It isn't a shadow. It has three dimensions. It is standing, facing me. As soon as I see it, I pause and stare. It is almost as if the shadow has been waiting for me to notice it. As soon as I do, it begins to fade and then dissolves into nothingness.

"Did you see?" I ask Mike.

He didn't, but I know what I saw. A three-dimensional man whose form was blacker than the black darkness of the snow shed quietly stood and waited to get my attention. As I pass off the end of the bridge of Area 61, I whisper a silent thank you. All I feel is peace.

I take one more trip down the snow shed with Larry, Leslie, and the kids. All is quiet, and as I walk, I silently bid farewell to my friends.

"I will be back," I tell them. "As soon as the snow clears, I will come."

After our last trip down the snow shed, we linger by the fire for a few more minutes before heading off to our hotel.

I am already feeling loss as I drive up the winding road away from Wellington and toward Highway 2. Thoughts of my summer at Wellington flash through my head, and I am filled with melancholy.

Finally, I reach Highway 2. As I take the turn, the weather tells me what I already know. I won't be coming back to Wellington until the spring. Just to make sure I know for certain that this is true, it begins to snow.

The Long Winter (January 11, 2010)

I awoke this morning to a dream of Wellington. I haven't been able to go in months, although Bert keeps me informed about the snow conditions there. The lower road is almost passable, he tells me. It only has three inches of snow on it.

While the snow came early this year, there hasn't been all that much. One hundred years after the horrible winter that led to the Wellington avalanche, the winter has been mild, as if in honor of the centennial of the disaster.

The good news, Bert tells me, is that this looks like a year where we'll get in earlier than ever.

I know I am not alone in how deeply I miss Wellington. The intensity of loss surprises me. I feel as if I am going through withdrawal. I feel as if I am grieving over long lost friends.

If it is this intense for me after one summer, I can only imagine how each winter must stretch ahead of Bert and Jayme. They love Wellington more than anyone I have ever met, and I know they regularly check to see how much longer they'll have to wait before they get through to Wellington again.

I thought having some breathing room might help me gain perspective. Instead, as I go about my days, I frequently feel a familiar energy. It always takes me a minute to recognize what is pulling at the corners of my mind, but then I remember. It is Wellington, and it is calling to   me.

There are many mornings when I wake from dreams of Wellington as I did this morning. I can feel it — just on the other side of my consciousness — awaiting my return.

Afterword

As I have indicated, there is no documentary. Due to creative differences with one of our documentary producers, we were not able to finish production. I just wanted to tell the story of a place I loved and respected, and I wanted the story to be a love letter to Wellington.

I could not, in good conscience, turn it into something forced and overly commercial.

It's okay though. Maybe this time around, the documentary just wasn't meant to be. That doesn't mean it will never be; it only means it isn't to be right now.

I've recovered from my overwhelming sadness of last November when the documentary first came to a screeching halt. I'm more philosophical now. Writing this book has been healing, because I've been able to return to Wellington in my heart and in my mind.

If I had to do it all over again, I can't say I would change a thing. Everything has worked out exactly as it should, and I am at peace with each of my actions and decisions along the way.

The 100-year anniversary of the avalanche disaster at Wellington is just a short month away as I write this: March 1, 2010. While we won't be releasing a documentary nor having a huge gathering to commemorate the loss of life at Wellington, as well as the loss of a town and a way of life, I will be there in my heart on March 1.

I'm usually an early-to-bed kind of gal, but I can't help but think that, in this case, I will be awake at 1:42 a.m. on March 1.

When that moment comes, will I hear a crack of thunder, a roar of snow, and the screams of the doomed, or will I merely feel a sense of longing and loss for such a beautiful and industrious place that was erased from the face of the Earth in the wake of unspeakable tragedy?

Karen Frazier
February 1, 2010

Update: 2012

As the end of August nears, I'm reminded I have just a few short months left at Wellington. Located as it is high in the North Cascade Mountains, Wellington is only accessible from late June/early July through late October/early November. Given the amount of snowfall in the past few years, we haven't been able to reach Wellington until July, and we have been done there by the end of October. In just a few weeks, verdant underbrush will give way to the burnt orange and bright red of fall foliage. Then, the snow will come once again, locking Wellington in an icy cage until the summer thaw.

Wellington remains my favorite place in the world. During the summer months, the stars shine brilliantly at night, with millions of points of light never   visible from the city. Along with stunning vistas of nearby peaks, the paths are lined with vibrant red castilleja (Indian paintbrush), purple foxglove, orange columbine, and wild strawberries. The air smells clean, and marmots call to one another from behind nearby rock outcroppings. This year, two juvenile barn owls have taken up residence in the forest alongside the snow shed. They converse in eerily screechy voices as the sun goes down.

I've written quite a lot about Wellington since I originally wrote *Avalanche of Spirits*. Every summer, I make multiple visits. In the past few months, my focus has been on introducing it to others — walking people through and sharing the history of the location and the haunting. I am blessed to be able to do so, since I believe the ghosts of Wellington want their story shared with as many people as possible. That is what I do, both onsite and off. I tell their story in the best way I know how.

Whenever I visit, I can feel the site reach out to embrace me. It is as if I am wrapped in the arms of old friends. No matter what's going on in my life, no matter how stressed I am, the second I set foot on that sacred site I am made whole. Everything fades away, and for however long I am there I achieve a state of Zen.

While Wellington feels familiar and friendly, it still has secrets to reveal. It is as if the town delights in showing me something new every single time I visit. This year, it is the addition of a tall, black, human-shaped mist that steps into my path, slowly fades away, and then reappears further off in the distance. This apparition beckons, leading me to whatever piece of the story he or she has to tell. Hopefully, it is a story I will know in full before winter sets in once again.

Another new experience is a giant presence called Bear. He stands so close, as if there is no personal space he is willing to let lie between us. He strokes my face and whispers in my ear, "You know me. You know me." He seems so certain I have to wonder if what he says is the truth. Perhaps I do. Perhaps in another life, another place, another time, I did know Bear the way he believes I do.

My relationship with Wellington has matured over the past several years. In the initial rush of new acquaintance, it was as if Wellington threw everything it had in an attempt to impress me. Now, it is more subtle yet meaningful. Today, Wellington opens up like a flower, revealing layer after subtle layer of its story.

The fireworks of that first heady summer at Wellington have given way to quieter phenomena. The children still rush to greet me, but now they do it silently, slipping their hand into mine as if to escort me about the site. The voices are quieter now. The touches are gentler. The apparitions are far softer and less defined. Perhaps it is because I no longer need the fireworks to believe, and so Wellington saves those for newcomers who have yet to give in to the town's charms.

Judging from the people who call and e-mail me, however, Wellington remains up to its old tricks, shocking newcomers with an aggressive and in-your-face campaign. When they return from their visit and inevitably find me somewhere in the ethers of the

Internet, those lucky enough to experience Wellington in all her haunted glory write me of loud voices, firm touches, bright lights, and solid apparitions. They are equal parts terrified and intrigued, and they want to share their story. I am happy to listen, overcome with nostalgia for the days when my relationship with Wellington was new, as well, and the town had much to show and tell me so I would believe and tell others.

I no longer investigate Wellington — I have no need to do so. When I go, my equipment remains either at home or in the car. Instead, I visit old friends. I sit quietly and listen. I walk and watch. And no matter what I see, hear, or experience, I always leave better than I was before I came.

Karen Frazier
August 23, 2012

Author's Note:

While all of the incidents described in *Avalanche of Spirits: The Ghosts of Wellington* are true, in some instances the names of people or paranormal teams have been changed.

In Memoriam

In memory of those who lost their lives in the biggest avalanche disaster in U.S. history, those who escaped but never forgot, and those who slowly watched their town die a silent and painful death. You will never be forgotten.

Avalanche Victims

Lee D. Ahern – mail weigher
Richard M. Barnhart – passenger
Erma Beck – passenger (child – age 4 1/2)
George Beck – passenger
Ella Beck – passenger
Harriet Beck – passenger (child – age 6)
Leonard Beck – passenger (child – age 2 3/4)
Grover W. Begle – express messenger
Earl Edgar Bennington – fireman
R.H. Bethel – passenger
John Bjart – laborer
John Bjerenson – waiter
Aurthur Reed Blackburn – trainmaster
Richard Clarence Bogart – mail clerk
Fred Bohn – mail weigher
Albert Boles – passenger
William Bovee – brakeman
John Brockman – passenger
Peter Bruno – laborer
Alex Campbell – rotary conductor
J.O. Carroll – engineer
H.D. Chantrell – passenger
Alex Chisholm – passenger
G. Christy – laborer
Ed Clark – railroader
Solomon Cohen – passenger
William Corcoran – engine watchman
Sarah Jane Covington – passenger
George Davis – passenger

Thelma Davis – passenger (child – age 3)
William Dorety – brakeman
Anthony Dougherty – brakeman
H.J. Drehl – express messenger
William Duncan – porter
Archie Dupy – brakeman
Harry Elerker – cook (killed in a slide at the Beanery a day earlier)
Charles Eltinge – passenger
Earl Fisher – fireman
Raymond Forsythe – passenger
John Fox – mail clerk
Inigi Giammarusti – laborer
Donald Gilman – electrician
Mike Guglielmo – laborer
George Heron – passenger
Milton Hicks – brakeman
George Hoefer – mail clerk
Benjamin Jarnagan – engineer
G.R. Jenks – fireman
Charles Jennison – brakeman
Sidney Jones – fireman
John Kelly – brakeman
William Kenzal – brakeman
Charles La Du – mail clerk
Libby Latsch – passenger
Sam Lee – passenger
Gus Leibert – laborer
Ada Lemman – passenger
Edgar Lemman – passenger
J. Liberati – laborer
Steven Lindsay – rotary conductor
Earl Longcoy – stenographer
John Mackie – passenger
Albert Mahler – passenger
Francis Martin – engineer
Bert Matthews – passenger
William May – passenger
Archibald McDonald – brakeman
Nellie McGirl – passenger
James McNeny – passenger
James Monroe – passenger

Peter Nino – engine watcher
Catherine O'Reilly – passenger
TL Osborne – engineer
Harry Partridge – fireman
John Parzybok – rotary conductor
Joseph Pettit – passenger conductor
Antonio Porlowlino – laborer
Donato Quarante – laborer (killed in a slide on 3-13)
William Raycroft – brakeman
L. Ross – fireman
Carl Smith – laborer
Francis Starrett – passenger (child – age 8 months)
Lillian Starrett – passenger (child – age 9)
Andrew Stohmier – brakeman
Vasily Suterin – laborer
Benjamin Thompson – passenger
Rev. James M. Thomson – passenger
Edward (Ned) Topping – passenger
Giovanni Tosti – laborer
Hiram Towslee – mail clerk
John Tucker – mail clerk
JR Vail – passenger
Lewis Walker – steward
GR Yerks – fireman
Unidentified #1 – laborer
Unidentified #2 – laborer
Unidentified #3 – laborer
Unidentified #4 – laborer
Unidentified #5 – laborer
Unidentified #6 – laborer

A Note About the Death Toll From the Wellington Avalanche

It is virtually impossible to know how many actually died in the Wellington avalanche. Published numbers swing anywhere from 96 up to around 120. There is some evidence that the Great Northern Railway (GNR), faced with a public relations disaster, made an effort to keep the published numbers as low as possible. They wanted to keep it fewer than 100.

There are a number of reasons why some victims may have not made the official death toll:

- The trains, locomotives, and rotaries swept away by the avalanche came to rest on a shelf above the Tye River. The weather warmed while rescue attempts were underway. There is speculation this led to a melting of the ice above the river, causing a number of bodies to fall through and drift downstream never to be found.

- The GNR was in the midst of labor difficulties. Several laborers walked off the job because they wanted more compensation for the backbreaking work that they were doing at Wellington. They believed that the conditions at Wellington put them in a very strong negotiating position, but the GNR felt very strongly they would not give in to extortion or blackmail and wouldn't budge on their wages. There is no record of how many laborers walked out and how many remained at Wellington.

Speculation is that many of the unknown and
unacknowledged dead were these laborers.

- In many cases, the GNR didn't know the name of the
  laborers, who received cash as wages. Many of these
  laborers were Italians, who, at the time, were considered
  to be almost sub-human. There are six unknowns on the
  list above — six unidentified workers. Speculation is that
  they were Italian laborers, and the railroad had never
  known their names, which is why they couldn't be
  identified. The initial estimated death toll came in at right
  around 120 — before bodies were recovered. There is a
  good chance that if the numbers were indeed this high,
  there were many more unnamed laborers who were left
  off the death rolls in order to make the number appear
  below 100.

Avalanche Survivors

John Gray – passenger
Anna Gray – passenger
Varden Gray – passenger (child age 18 months)
RM Laville – passenger
Mrs. William May – passenger
Ida Starrett – passenger
Raymond Starrett – passenger (child age 7)
Henry White – passenger
Lucius Anderson – porter
Samuel Bates – fireman
Ira Clary – rotary conductor
ES Duncan – brakeman
Ray Forsyth, laborer
William Harrington – trainmaster
Alfred Hensel – mail clerk
J.L. Kerlee – brakeman
George Nelson – fireman
Homer Purcell – rotary conductor
Ross Phillips – brakeman
Adolph Smith – porter
Irving Tegtmeier – master mechanic
M.O. White – rotary conductor

Passengers and Employees Who Hiked to Safety

John Merritt – passenger
Lewis Jesseph – passenger
George Loveberry – passenger
John Rogers – passenger
E.A. Sperber – passenger
R. McKnight – passenger
Charles Young – passenger
Frank Ritter – passenger
E.W. Boles – passenger
Samuel Field – passenger
H.L. Mertz – railway employee
Angus Van Larke – railroad employee
Guiseppe Dinatale – laborer

About the Town of Wellington

In what was once a bustling railroad town where people built their lives and grew their families amidst rugged mountains peaks, there now sits a parking lot and the crumbling foundations of a few of the buildings that had once been there. Sadly, the town of Wellington died as violent a death as did the people in the trains lost in avalanches and other railroad disasters at Wellington.

After the avalanche, the GNR wanted to remove the tragedy from the public psyche as quickly as possible. The name Wellington had become synonymous with death and disaster. The railroad quietly renamed the town Tye, and it remained intact for another 20 years until the GNR built a new Cascade Tunnel with new tracks lower in the mountains. When the railroad went away, the town slowly disappeared.

I would also like to remember and acknowledge those brave souls who built their lives in such a breathtakingly beautiful, yet harsh, location. They, too, endured unimaginable tragedy as they watched the town they had built, lived in, and loved fade away to nothingness. Their sacrifice is no less noble than those who died in the avalanche disasters.

If one looks at the U.S. Census reports from 1900–1930, you will see that the population slowly dwindled until the GNR opened the new, lower elevation track in Scenic in 1929 and the railroad no longer went through Wellington.

"Perhaps they are not the stars but rather openings in the

heavens where the love of our lost ones pours through and

shines down upon us to let us know they are happy."

~Eskimo Proverb

Acknowledgements

So many have participated and helped me as I've researched Wellington from the very beginning. It is difficult to begin to know where to start. That's why I will start with this. Thank you everyone who has shared Wellington with me, as well as those who have allowed me to share Wellington with them. It is a special group that Wellington has drawn to itself, and each of you have become an important part of its story.

In particular, I'd like to thank the following people:

1. My husband Jim, you are a darn good sport to chase your wife around in the wilderness for two years, spend thousands on a film never made, and serve as an amazing support system.

2. Tanner and Kevin, you're terrific kids and I can only hope we haven't bored the crap out of you with all this Wellington stuff.

3. Jayme Coates, you've been a wonderful supporter, a terrific friend, a mentor, and as always, you are a spectacular photographer. Thanks for all of those.

4. Bert Coates, I appreciate your support, your knowledge, and your willingness to share your special place with a couple of upstarts from down south.

5. Without Shane Bodiford's amazing picture, I would have never known Wellington existed. Shane, you're a great friend, a good investigator, and I'm glad to know you. Thank you.

6. To the members of all the teams who have shared Wellington, thank you, including NWPIA, West Coast Ghost Hunters, Cascade Paranormal, RIP Paranormal, and Ghost Hunters of Washington. Also, thanks to all of the people I've connected with at or about Wellington. It's nice to feel a part of such a rich and diverse community.

7. I'll always appreciate the members of WAR for taking me to Wellington the first time.

8. Cheryl Knight and Chad Wilson at Ghost Knight Media and Paranormal Underground have been tremendously supportive, good friends, and great editors. Thank you.

9. To my on-air partner Rick Hale, thanks for letting me use our show time to yammer on about Wellington. Hopefully you can get here soon.

10. Everyone who has e-mailed me photos, evidence, and stories, thanks! Thank you also to everyone who has e-mailed me about the book and shared your feedback. It means a great deal.

11. Thanks to all of the radio hosts, event organizers, and television producers who have allowed me to continue to

tell the ongoing story of Wellington.

About the Author

Karen Frazier is the former Managing Editor and a current writer for *Paranormal Underground* magazine. In that capacity, she's written articles about a number of paranormal topics, including UFOs, ghosts, paranormal investigation, reincarnation, and many others. She also hosted and produced Paranormal Underground's podcast, *Paranormal Underground Presents,* and currently serves as the co-host of *Paranormal Underground Radio.* Karen also served as the site editor and a writer for *LoveToKnow Paranormal,* where she wrote paranormal articles, conducted interviews, and provided advice to people seeking help. She is currently an investigator for South Sound Paranormal Research.

In addition to *Avalanche of Spirits,* Karen co-wrote *Lessons of Many Lives* with Melissa Watts.

Karen lives in the Pacific Northwest with her husband, two sons, and four dogs. She currently works as a freelance writer, volunteers as a court-appointed special advocate for children, and provides volunteer outreach for the Crisis Clinic of Thurston and Mason Counties. She is working on a follow-up to *Avalanche of Spirits: The Ghosts of Wellington,* updating all of the amazing events that continue to unfold during her time at Wellington.

For more information, visit her Website at www.karenfrazier.com.

Dancing with the Afterlife: A Paranormal Memoir

The story continues.

In the follow-up to *Avalanche of Spirits: The Ghosts of Wellington*, Paranormal Underground Radio's Karen Frazier picks up where she left off, expanding her recent experiences at Wellington into ongoing research about afterlife.

Even as a child, Karen found herself drawn to topics of the soul. Throughout her adulthood, she's sought answers to a single question: "Does consciousness survive death?"

In *Dancing with the Afterlife: A Paranormal Memoir* Karen shares the experiences she had that first spurred her curiosity, and later led her search.

Touching on topics including ghosts, reincarnation, life between lives, psychic ability, and near-death experiences, Karen shares how her time as a paranormal and afterlife researcher has led her to the inescapable conclusion consciousness survives bodily death.

Want to Know More?

See and hear much of the evidence discussed in this book at

WellingtonProject.Org

Visit the author's website

KarenFrazier.com

Visit the *Avalanche of Spirits* website

AvalancheOfSpirits.com

Enjoy an excerpt from Karen Frazier's new book:

Dancing with the Afterlife: A Paranormal Memoir

On the following pages

FOREWORD

Everyone's got a story to tell, and I suppose I'm no different. I already shared much of my story in my 2010 book, *Avalanche of Spirits: The Ghosts of Wellington.* When I wrote the book, only part of it was about me. The rest was about the spirits at Wellington: people killed in an avalanche, people who lived in the town and loved it, and people who completed backbreaking work on the railroad in harsh conditions, earning just enough to pay from the railroad for a place to sleep with a few pennies left over for whiskey.

It's fair to say the spirits of those people have haunted me since I first visited Wellington in the summer of 2009. They had a story, and they wanted it told. I always felt I was merely a scribe – a person with a computer and a basic command of the English language – who could help them tell their tale. I've always believed *Avalanche* came from them, through me – not from me.

Of course, *Avalanche* was just a little bit about me, too. Part of the book was my memoir. It was the story of a woman whose life was changed by an encounter with a ghost town filled with spirits. It was about my relationship with the ghosts at Wellington, who I grew to love. It was the story of a little boy named Leonard who captured my heart, as well as a number of nameless (and often faceless) spirits who became family.

I wrote *Avalanche of Spirits* in the winter of 2009. During that time, the snow had come to the mountains, and I couldn't venture up to Wellington. I was feeling cut off and a little empty. At the time, I believed physical proximity to Wellington was essential to communication with the spirits there. I was feeling, for lack of a better term, homesick.

Since I first visited Wellington back in 2009, and since the book released in March of 2010 to coincide with the 100-year anniversary of the Wellington avalanche that claimed so many lives, I have told the story countless times. I've told it on the radio, in television segments, and at conferences. I've shared photographs, history, and EVPs. I've led tours of the site to interested visitors. I've had private and public conversations about Wellington. I've been interviewed for blogs and publications. It has been my goal to share their story because it is what the spirits at Wellington indicated they wanted me to do. Wellington has become a solid chunk of my life's work. It has been my joy and privilege to tell the tale, introducing the spirits there to a curious and compassionate public who seem to respond to their story in very personal and intimate ways.

When I finished writing *Avalanche*, I thought that was the end of it. Sure, I still intended to visit the spirits at Wellington, and I knew I would continue to share their tale, but I thought that was where my story with Wellington ended. I believed my task was complete, because I had done (and continued to do) what I promised. I never imagined I would revisit Wellington again with another book. Instead, I assumed another haunted place or a different subject would grab ahold of me, and off I'd go in a different direction.

However, I've learned life is never what I expect it to be. Certainly that is the way of things with Wellington. It turns out Wellington remains my story. When others visit and experience the spirits there, it becomes their story, as well.

There is much more to be told, it seems. The spirits there have more to say, and they aren't shy about asking me to pass it on to others. They make no bones about the fact they are not done with me. They tell me their story continues and so does my involvement in it. While they are almost ready to move on, they first want me to tell you more. They want me to tell you how their story is a small part of a much larger truth. They want me to hold nothing back. And so, because they insist, the narrative continues.

PART I: BACKSTORY
(1965-2009)

2012: ONE TRICK PONY

I was starting to feel like a one trick pony. In March of 2010, I published *Avalanche of Spirits: The Ghosts of Wellington*. The book was a hastily written memoir of my first summer at Wellington – the site of the worst avalanche disaster in the history of the United States.

After publishing *Avalanche* and participating in the whirlwind of promotional activity and speaking engagements that followed, my ego suggested to me I was done with Wellington (except for going back to continue to visit the spirits there). I thought I'd probably move on to the next book project.

People began asking me just what I had planned for my next book. My answer was always the same: "I need to fall in love with a subject in order to write about it."

I kept waiting to fall in love, but lightning never struck. Wellington stayed with me. It appears I was not yet ready to move on.

Instead of plunging headlong into a new book project, I went back and created an enhanced version of the old one – complete with a brief video introduction and access to all the electronic data files (electronic voice phenomena, photo evidence, etc.) I discussed in *Avalanche*. Maybe this would finally help me shake Wellington loose and move onto my next book.

With the enhanced iBook published, I waited for the next subject I could write about with passion. I had nothing. Instead, Wellington remained, pulling at me stronger than ever before. The spirits of Wellington were louder and more insistent than they had ever been.

While Wellington remained a major focus for me, I also moved forward with a number of other activities, mostly having to do with afterlife research. I dug through data, publications, and files of scientific afterlife researchers like Dr. Gary E. Schwartz, Dr. Raymond Moody, Dr. Michael Newton, Dr. Brian Weiss, and the Society for Psychical Research. I was determined to find the place where science and the paranormal intersect.

As I delved into the afterlife, I also dug more deeply into Wellington until the two arrived at a confluence. They intertwined until I could no longer separate them.

Wellington, it seems, is the lynchpin for me. It is the most important part of a larger whole. It's not so much I am a one trick pony as it is I haven't reached the bottom of the well that is Wellington just yet. Instead of allowing my intellect to continue to lead me, I need to listen to my intuition.

Thus it begins again, as I dig deeper than I ever have before for answers about why I feel it matters so much.

JANUARY 23, 2013: DISSATISFACTION

I've been noticing a prickly feeling of dissatisfaction lately. It's like a psychic itch – a sense of discomfort that tells me I need to do something. As I always do, I first try ignoring it. Maybe it's something I ate or lack of sleep.

I should know better by now. Ignoring the itch never works for me. Instead, as it always does, it grows stronger by the moment. The feeling I need to pay attention takes on increasing density, as if my consciousness must claw its way through viscous liquid. Every moment, the sensation is harder to ignore until I finally can't anymore. I quit trying and start to pay attention.

As soon as I do, I feel a familiar tickle -- the recognition of an energy I know intimately. It is the energy of the collective group of spirits I've come to know so well at Wellington, and their message is loud and clear. It's time to tell the story. The whole story.

People often ask what I mean when I say I feel the pull of Wellington. Is it a physical sensation? Do I see or hear something? The truth is, it is something very difficult to define using words, even for someone who earns her living as a writer. Wellington's spirits are a feeling. It's not necessarily an emotion, and it's not quite physical. Instead, the collective of spirits come to me as a signature sensation. It's like a tickle to my psyche that is familiar, yet completely unique. I don't know if this is something only I experience or if it works for others, as well, but I sense everyone energetically – both living and dead.

Every person emits a signature feeling – a vibration. Like snowflakes, no two are alike. I can differentiate between those vibrations. When someone enters my presence and I don't see him or her, I often know who it is anyway by that sensation. I will feel a person's essence moments before I receive a phone call, email, or text.

If I tune into that vibration, I can give you a physical location where I notice it. It is on my right side, slightly above my ear, at a point hovering just outside of my head. Sometimes there is an emotion or a physical sensation attached, as well. That is how the collective group of spirits at Wellington comes to me, and they are highly recognizable. Individual spirits also come. Each has both the signature of the collective I've come to recognize as Wellington, as well as their own, unique essence. For me, each is easily discernable from the others.

Now they are here as a collective, telling me I need to finish what I started by telling the entire story.

1965 TO 1987: KEEPING SECRETS

For most of my life, I considered my struggle with faith to be one of my defining characteristics. I grew up in a fairly liberal branch of the Christian church – the United Church of Christ. As a youth and a teenager, church was a constant presence in my life. I attended Sunday school every week. When I was old enough, I joined the youth group.

Many of my high school friends were in the Christian clique. With my church background, I could fit in quite seamlessly. The problem was, I was harboring a secret. While everyone around me seemed to believe in Biblical stories and have faith in the Christian God, I was only paying it lip service. Instead of being filled with faith and hope at the message of Christianity, I was riddled with doubt. Bible stories didn't make a whole lot of sense to me, but it was easier to follow along than speak up. I watched the unshakable faith of those around me and hoped some of it would rub off on me.

It wasn't that I didn't believe in God. In a sense I did. However, the God I envisioned wasn't some jealous petty tyrant who punished people because they didn't prostrate themselves at His feet. Instead, God was more an underlying source – an intelligence that ran through all of life. God wasn't a guy in the sky. It was the creativity and beauty all around us. God was the breath and life of the universe.

At the same time, I was fascinated by ghost stories. I voraciously read paranormal fiction because I was completely fascinated with the idea of ghosts. While ghosts might make a great fiction subject, however, I knew they weren't real. At least I thought I knew.

As I entered college, my religious agnosticism morphed into full-fledged atheism. Not only did I not believe in God, I decided, but I was pretty sure human beings didn't have souls.

Ironically, this self-identification of atheism, which I felt was a very reasoned, rational, and scientific belief, pushed me further into the supernatural. Suddenly anything having to do with the afterlife enthralled me. I started reading books about reincarnation, psychic abilities, and similar topics.

Reincarnation particularly interested me, although if humans didn't have souls, I wasn't really sure how it could be a real thing. One of my most vivid memories of being a teen, however, was a dream I had when I was about 16. In the dream, I was me, but not me. I lived in the woods and protected my young siblings and a foreign soldier. We were hiding from some unknown enemy and speaking a language my waking self didn't recognize. The dream was different than any other I'd ever had. It seemed hyper-real. It was so vivid, it remains with me to this day.

When I told my dad about the dream he said, "Maybe what you saw was a past life."

It sparked my intense interest in reincarnation, which became another secret subject of study.

OCTOBER 1987: WIDE AWAKE AT THE SUPER 8

When I was 21, I left college and married my high school sweetheart. He was a nuclear electronics technician (a "nuke") stationed aboard a submarine at the Naval Submarine Base Bangor in Washington State. We moved into a tiny apartment in East Bremerton that had been WWII naval officers' housing.

My husband, David, spent three months at a time out to sea aboard a Trident nuclear submarine. While he was gone, I was alone in the apartment. It was the first time I'd lived completely by myself, without parents, siblings, roommates, or dorm dwellers all around me. While I was proud to be living alone, the nights in that tiny apartment really freaked me out.

It started simply enough with things that went bump in the night. One night shortly after David deployed, I was in the bedroom reading. I heard a soft click in our kitchen, followed by a thunk. I got up and peeked out my bedroom door and into the kitchen (it was a very tiny apartment). I noticed a latched cupboard door had come open. The first click was the latch, and the thunk was the door reaching its full open capacity. Breathing a sigh of relief, I went and closed the cupboard. As I walked away, there was another click and thunk behind me. I turned, and a different cupboard door was standing open. I closed it and went to bed. That night, I slept with the bathroom light on. I also turned on the radio next to the bed so I wouldn't have to hear anything else.

A few nights later, I was in my living room when I heard the creak of our bathroom faucet. Then, water started splashing into the basin. Suspecting I was hearing the guy upstairs, I checked the bathroom. Water ran in the sink. My entire body was overcome with chills.

That night, I was in a hyper-vigilant state when I went to bed. As I lay in the dark with my eyes tightly closed and my back to the door, I heard the sound of soft footsteps that started near my front door. The footsteps walked across the hardwood floor, through my bedroom door, and to the side of my bed.

I was paralyzed. While my body felt as if it couldn't move, my mind was racing – rationalizing what I was really hearing was the guy upstairs coming home.

Then the mattress next to me depressed as if someone sat on the edge of my bed.

A voice whispered in my ear, "I love you."

I could feel moist breath on my cheek. My hair fluttered as if someone truly was whispering in my ear.

Adrenaline surged, and I broke through my paralysis. I sprang out of bed and turned on the light. Carefully searching every nook and cranny of the apartment, I realized there was no one there. I told myself it was just a dream. Then I called a local Super 8 motel to see if they had vacancy, grabbed a few things for work the next day, and fled the apartment. I spent the night wide-awake in the Super 8.

I didn't return home to my apartment until after work the next afternoon. I was exhausted from my sleepless night, and I planned to take a nap before teaching my 6:00 p.m. aerobics class at a nearby gym. I told myself I'd have no trouble sleeping during the daytime, especially given my present state of exhaustion.

When I arrived at my apartment, I cautiously peeked through the front door. I was surprised to see the hall closet door open and blocking the view into my bedroom. Telling myself I must've opened the closet door in my terror-filled flight from my apartment the night before, I closed it and jumped a mile high. A six-foot tall inflatable green Godzilla, the questionable decorating choice of my young sailor husband, was somehow sitting on the middle of my bed. Normally, it resided in a corner of our living room, just behind the television set. Now, there it sat atop my mattress, its plastic reptilian eyes mocking my fear.

In my kitchen, the cupboard doors all stood open. Water ran in the sink. I made a beeline out the front door and down to the apartment manager's office.

"Has anyone been in my apartment today?" I asked the

162

manager.

She looked baffled and scratched her head. "No," she told me. "We won't enter without your permission, and if we have to come in for an emergency, we'll leave a note."

"I think I've had a break-in, then." I told her. I explained what I'd found.

"Was your front door unlocked?" she asked. "Any windows open, broken, or other points of entry?"

We returned to my apartment and found it had, indeed, been buttoned up tight. The manager suggested I call the police. I can't remember why I chose not to, but I didn't. Instead, I returned home and locked myself in, checking every door and window several times to make sure they were secure. They were.

David and I were near penniless in those days, and I knew I couldn't afford to stay at the Super 8 every night until he returned from sea in a few months. Instead I did what I considered the next best thing. I got two cats.

I began sleeping at night with the lights shining, the television on, and the radio playing next to my bed. When I crawled in bed after checking the front door and every window in the place several times, I would pull my comforter up over my head so only the part in my hair stuck out. I surrounded myself with pillows so nobody could get to me. Every night, I tried to bring the cats into my bedroom. As soon as their feet hit the mattress, they'd bolt and curl up on the living room couch. They were having none of the bedroom, period.

In spite of my protections, something in that apartment continued to haunt me. Some nights, the "I love you" spirit would visit me. On others, the water would turn on in the bathroom. Sometimes, it was just latched doors and cupboards that would open and close. All the while, I would lie under my comforter with my eyes squeezed tightly shut, telling myself it wasn't happening. I was certain it was just my imagination on overdrive because I was living alone.

When my husband came home from sea, I begged him to move. Before he deployed the next time, we were living in a new apartment on the other side of town.

Want to read more? The book is now available!

DancingWithTheAfterlife.com

Printed in Great Britain
by Amazon